WORDS INTO CA$H

WORDS
INTO
CA$H

BLOG YOUR WAY

OUT OF THE

RAT RACE AND INTO

SECURE, STABLE

FINANCIAL FREEDOM

TIMOTHY S. KIM

LIONCREST
PUBLISHING

WORDS INTO CASH

Blog Your Way out of the Rat Race and into Secure, Stable Financial Freedom

ISBN   978-1-5445-1216-7 *Paperback*
       978-1-5445-1215-0 *Ebook*
       978-1-5445-1217-4 *Audiobook*

CONTENTS

INTRODUCTION

How much money did you make while you were sleeping last night?

Sound like a stupid question? It's not, because I made a little over $900 while in a full-fledged REM state of deep sleep last night. Some nights, I make more; some nights, I make less, but last month, I made about $30,000.

Don't believe me? I don't blame you, but just google my name and you'll see that I've been featured on CNBC, Business Insider, Huffington Post, and many other national news outlets, as well as over a dozen radio programs. In fact, most of these media sources required a background check and a fairly rigorous audit, just to ensure that my numbers weren't subject to any sort of "creative interpretation."

Now, what if I said that I could show you how to earn just as much—or more—with your own passive income while sleeping just as soundly? I assure you that this is no get-rich-quick scheme either.

The truth is, you can make enough money while sleeping, practicing Brazilian jiujitsu, playing World of Warcraft, or just spending time with friends and family to quit the nine-to-five rat race, and enjoy a carefree lifestyle of total autonomy.

All you need to do is commit your time and effort to a simple activity of the technological age—blogging. The strangest thing of all is that many of you may already be doing this, but you probably think of it as more of a hobby than anything else, which is fine, but it won't generate any extra income for you, and it definitely won't allow you to quit your day job.

By treating your blog like a modern business and incorporating social media for audience growth, you won't have to wait for the old school, more traditional methods of blogging to monetize.

This has been a key element to my success, and I can tell you how to do it too. That's right; keep reading, and I'll tell you how to quickly turn your words into cash, just like I did.

BLOGGING EQUALS SMART MONEY

After reading this book, you're going to have a distinct advantage over all the veteran bloggers who have been doing this for over a decade. They're focusing on the wrong thing, and honestly, most of them still aren't making a lot of money.

My blog—tubofcash.com—earns income in several ways, which will all be discussed in full detail later on, but an affiliate partnership is one of the most significant of all the potential income earners. Most high-earning bloggers have between three and five affiliate partners. I have only one, which means I'm barely scratching the surface of the money I can really make.

At the end of the month, however, the income I earn from that single affiliate program will still be somewhere between $5,000 and $10,000. Although I'm quite satisfied with that amount, it's comforting to know that I could earn much more if I really wanted to.

You might think that earning money by blogging is crazy complicated or requires a lot of hard work, but it's neither of those things. Actually, it's embarrassingly easy to do! In fact, I encourage just about everybody to do it because it's that simple. For an example that proves my point, just compare how much easier it is to earn a lot of money from blogging as opposed to working a fairly common corporate job, like sales.

Even the most naturally gifted and vastly experienced salespeople in the world usually have to make a hundred or more cold calls to get a single sale. Meanwhile, I can post one blog that earns money for as long as people read it. In that sense, it may not be 100 percent passive income, because I do have to write the blog, but that's all I have to do.

The work is front-loaded, and the blog post only takes about thirty minutes to write. My work is done after that, and that single post could continue earning money through affiliate programs and ad networks for many days, weeks, months, and even years to come!

None of the income streams from blogging involve as much work as being a traditional salesperson or any corporate job I can think of, and I should know because I've been there and done that too.

FROM NEAR POVERTY IN SOUTH KOREA TO MILLIONAIRE IN LOS ANGELES

At this point, you may be wondering if I'm some know-it-all, rich kid who has never worked an honest day in his life. The answer is no. I know quite well what it's like to work very hard and get by with very little.

No, I haven't spent the last ten years sipping lattes and pounding on my MacBook Air keyboard while fusion jazz either infuriates or delights the rest of the patrons in the background. Isn't that the vision most people have of a career blogger? I've come to success from much further than just the local trendy coffee shop. I've come from almost the other side of the world.

I was born in South Korea, and I lived with my family in the capital city of Seoul until I was five years old. The median household income and standard of living there isn't too far behind the United States, but the atmosphere, particularly where we lived, left a lot to be desired. South Korea in the 1980s wasn't anything like the booming economical nation and entertainment mecca it is today. It was definitely not...Gangnam style!

Seoul is only about twenty to thirty miles from the North Korean border, so living there means you get used to having artillery aimed in the general direction of your home at all times. Psychologically, that's just a little more unsettling than having to deal with the preposterous traffic jams and overpriced pizza of life in Los Angeles.

For better or worse, my parents—who were missionaries—moved to Hungary with my brother and me in 1991, which was the same year that the last of the Soviet troops left the country. In all my years growing up in post-communist

Eastern Europe, I don't think I ever ran into another Asian family. That sort of isolation can be very challenging for anybody, young or old.

In those days, Hungary was very mono-ethnic. The country was almost exclusively made up of native Hungarians and a fair smattering of Roma—people with no country of their own—but there were zero Asians (other than my family) as far as I knew.

Actually, there was one more group of people that lived there as well—the neo-Nazis. Overall, Hungary just wasn't a supportive atmosphere to foreigners in those days. There was a lot of ignorance and hatred in that environment, and I wouldn't wish it on my worst enemy. Thankfully, times are much different there now.

Finally, when I was eighteen years old, I immigrated to the United States to go to school with nothing more than $500 in my pocket. I graduated from college and quickly began my corporate experience, working for a midsized wholesale garage automation distributor. I started in the warehouse, making around twelve dollars an hour, which wouldn't have been too bad in South Korea or Hungary, but it wasn't so great in Southern California.

I had zero connections when I started working in the warehouse there, but I gutted it out, mostly because I had no other choice. Eventually, I worked my way out of the warehouse and began to climb the corporate ladder. It was a nine-year ascension that ended with me serving as the vice president of procurement for the company.

Life as an executive wasn't something I loved, however. I got up at 5 o'clock every morning and worked mostly twelve-hour days. I also worked weekends and performed various side hustles as a personal trainer and in other capacities, which amounted to mostly seventy- to eighty-hour workweeks, so I hardly ever spent quality time with my wife and child, nor did I get to do much of the other things I liked.

Eventually, I had enough and quit. I remained on good terms with everybody there, but I just wasn't happy with the day-to-day grind, so I left.

"What, are you crazy?" you might be asking, while wondering how I was going to take care of my family.

You aren't alone, if that's what you're thinking. In fact, just about all my relatives and in-laws thought I was completely crazy to leave what they saw as a "cushy" job for something they couldn't understand.

Blogging and social media is extremely foreign to a lot of people, especially first-generation immigrants who only know one way to make money—traditional, hard work and plenty of it.

I wasn't crazy though, because I had already found a way to escape the daily rigor without losing income. In fact, the free time I was going to gain by leaving my corporate role would free up enough time for me to make much more money.

These days, I get to do what I want, and when I want to do it. There is no boss for me to answer to, and I set all the expectations. The typical Monday-through-Friday drudgery is gone. Every day is like Saturday as a blogger. Of course, I choose to work most Saturdays, but that's because I like what I do so much.

I'm incredibly thankful that I found a way out of the corporate grind and into the passive-income lifestyle, and that's what I want to do for you now. I don't have any special skills that make me uniquely suited for success with blogging. The only thing I've done differently is that I've never been caught up in best practices. I'll dive a little deeper into that thought later in the book, but for now, just understand that it's key to try things nobody else is doing.

I was also never a great student, so it's not like I'm some sort of whiz kid composing maniacally sophisticated algorithms in my garage while building the next great piece of tech gear. Considering the ultimate freedom and substantial income I've achieved through blogging despite my less than extraordinary background, I'm certain anyone can do this.

After all, I'm really just an ordinary, thirty-one-year-old guy who wasn't happy settling for the traditional career path, and I don't think you should either, because the traditional career path may not be around for much longer.

JOB INSECURITY IN THE NEW ECONOMY

The economy in the United States and most other developed nations is drastically changing. Traditional, forty-year corporate gigs with pensions, great benefits, and casual Fridays including pizza parties in the breakroom are fading away. Those roles are steadily becoming ghosts of the global economy's pre-technological past. The passive-income and multi-gig lifestyle is taking center stage as the new world economy plays out for millennials of today and future generations of tomorrow.

Artificial intelligence (AI), automation, and other cutting-edge technologies are the biggest contributors to the disappearing traditional career path. Recent studies by various reputable research firms and prominent futurists like Ray Kurzweil (currently Director of Engineering at Google) and Elon Musk (CEO and Founder of Tesla and SpaceX) have shown that as much as half of the job market will be completely replaced by AI and automation in the next twenty years.

My guess is that it might happen much sooner and potentially be even more severe than that. I also think that people are in for another surprise related to those numbers. Most people think the blue-collar jobs in warehouses and factories are the only ones that are going to vanish. However, I think that even more white-collar jobs will be affected.

Anything that's repetitive will be done by a machine in the coming years, so packing materials on an assembly line is certainly an at-risk job, but so is sitting at a desk, crunching numbers for an accounting ledger, and many other high-paying executive jobs.

Human workers have limitations. Corporations need to pay significant salaries and benefits to assembly workers, accountants, and other employees on all rungs of the corporate ladder. Additionally, these workers can only work so many hours in a day. Meanwhile, robots and software don't need to be paid anything more than the upfront cost to acquire them and some associated routine maintenance. They also don't need benefits, and they can work twenty-four hours per day, seven days per week, with no coffee or bathroom breaks.

In addition to the threats posed by technology to eliminate jobs, it's also becoming increasingly difficult and highly competitive to land a corporate job to begin with. I've seen thousands of resumés and conducted countless interviews from my days as a VP in the corporate grind. One thing I remember is that the competition was frighteningly fierce, whether it was a senior buyer position at stake or an entry-level job in the warehouse.

Usually, hundreds of people would apply, most of them with MBAs; the candidates who didn't have an advanced degree got their resumés thrown in the trash before the process even began in earnest. A lot of the MBAs didn't have any real-world experience, so those resumes went in the trash as well. The candidates who remained then needed to find some way to separate themselves from the massive herd of other equally qualified candidates, which was not easy.

Ultimately, a career choice is yours. You can be one of those hundred-plus candidates vying for the same corporate job that may pay $50,000–$75,000 per year, which could be eliminated by AI at any given moment. Or, you can fully embrace the future by reaping the rewards of blogging as a business.

If you treat your blog like a business, not a hobby, your income will most likely exceed that of a typical corporate job in less than a year-and-a-half. Not only will your income grow, but so will your personal life because you'll be your own boss with much more free time at your disposal.

WHAT THIS BOOK IS AND IS NOT

This book is not a step-by-step, technical guide for how to start a blog. You can easily find that information on Google or YouTube if you need it. You might even be able to ask a buddy or two how it's done. In fact, a simple Google search for "How do I start a blog?" will probably yield about ten thousand results—maybe more. Therefore, you don't need me or my book for that information.

From my corporate background, education, and mentorship, I've learned a lot about marketing, business, psychology, and social media, which is where my advice in this book will help you the most.

If you've read the CNBC article about me, you know that I spend around $12,000 per month on elite mentors and coaches. They're world-class business people whom I get my information from. These expenditures can also be verified by the fact that I had to provide actual invoices and statements related to this investment for CNBC to publish anything.

I can tell you how to create income streams and how to treat your blog like a business. More specifically, you're going to learn how to incorporate nuanced business concepts, disregard old-world best practices, and truly harness the immense power and reach of social media in the modern technological age.

Furthermore, this book will explain—in an extremely conversational, easy-to-understand manner—everything you need to know to get started on a lifestyle of passive income through blogging.

If you're already blogging, great! In that case, you'll learn how to transform your personally satisfying hobby into a remarkably thriving business with a global reach. If you're an excited newbie, that's great too! You'll learn about the new possibilities that await.

Either way, it's time for you to get to work. Move on to Chapter One, which will explain exactly how much time you will need to invest to make the income you'd like to achieve in return. A quick preview: you probably don't need to invest nearly as much time as you currently think you do.

RISK LITTLE FOR BIG RETURNS

Most people think that blogging for income is a gamble—like you have to hit the lottery to make any real money with it. They look at my success as a blogger as if I unwittingly struck gold on some unforeseen, incredibly nuanced subject matter that millions of people around the world had an insatiable appetite for. Or people think, "Well, he just got lucky. That would never work again, not for me anyway." But, that's not what happened.

I get it; it's hard to believe that something so simple could be so lucrative, but it can be, and the best part is you've got nothing to lose!

What happens if you go all-in on a blogging business and

fail? Do the blogging police come to your home and seize all your assets? What about prison time, bankruptcy, permanent damage to your reputation? No, none of those things happen. Your credit score doesn't even take a hit. In the blogosphere, there is a mere microcosm of risk to assume, with a world of riches to gain.

Personally, I like to experiment a lot. If there's only a little risk involved of potential failure, why not go for it? Truthfully, the only legitimate risk involved is that your blog doesn't work. For some reason, people tend to catastrophize their failures, but I see them as nothing more than experiments.

FAILURE...WHAT'S THE BIG DEAL?

There's an old business adage that encourages entrepreneurs and others seeking long-term success to "Fail fast; Fail often." With that in mind, I like to move from idea to execution in very little time, and I suggest you take the same approach. The faster you can act on an idea, the faster you'll successfully execute on one of them. It's a lot like taking half-court shots in basketball. Keep shooting, and eventually one of them is going to fall in the hoop.

Failure is such an ominous word. People react to it like it's the monster who's been hiding under their bed since they were young children. As a result, people tend to over-plan everything, especially business ventures. This over-planning is fed by procrastination, which is disguised as "due diligence" when a fearful mindset is present. The fearful mindset responds to the idea of a blogging business by saying something like, "Oh, I need to look into that more deeply. I don't know if I'm ready to blog yet." Not ready yet, really?

That makes no sense to me. I can think of only two reasons why somebody wouldn't be ready to blog:

1. They just don't want to. (Maybe you hate writing...or money.)
2. They can't read or write. (Believe it or not, an estimated 26 percent of the world is thought to be non-literate.)

For that matter, if you can't write or just don't like it, you can still video blog (vlog)!

If neither of these is true of you, why wait? There's almost zero investment involved, so delaying is just an unnecessary obstacle you're putting in front of your success. It's procrastination disguised as due diligence.

Blogging is not a binding agreement for anything. The worst thing that can happen is that maybe you pay for a year of web hosting and don't get a lot of return on investment (ROI), so you may be out a couple hundred dollars, at most.

Truthfully, you don't even need to invest that much, because WordPress is around $99 per year and Blogger. com is free. There's also free hosting available if you're willing to endure other companies making money from publishing ads to your site. So, you can start your blog with zero financial risk if you prefer.

Although, there's something wrong if you can't come up with $100-$200 to invest, because even the average homeless person makes around $13 per hour while walking a street corner with a freshly penned, "Help Me!" sign around their neck. Actually, substantiated accounts claim some *elite* panhandlers in New York City make over $100,000 a year. Try not to think about that one too much.

The point is—trust me, you can come up with the money if you need to. If not, you probably don't have the grit it takes to succeed in your own business anyway.

I'll talk more about hosting services later, but for now, just know that they don't require a significant, if any, investment.

HOW *NOT* TO FAIL

If you fail, you're going to easily recover from whatever miniscule investment you put into your blogging business, and your reputation isn't going to be damaged just because you started a blog that didn't make you a millionaire.

Still, nobody *wants* to fail. Everybody has different goals. Some—like myself—may want to make enough money to quit their day job and enjoy a total passive-income lifestyle. Others may just want to make a nice, little supplemental income. Therefore, the question becomes how do you accomplish your goals, whatever they are? In other words, how do you not experience an epic fail in your blogging business?

There are going to be three key points for you to remember to answer that question. Maybe take a highlighter to this section. It might serve as a handy reference point later on while you're making progress on your business. The three points are as follows:

1. Monetize early.
2. Don't stress about the content.
3. Find your customers.

MONETIZE EARLY

Full disclosure...I like blogging. It's fun for me, but I don't think I'm a lot different from most of the internet-using world in that regard. Blogging can be a great hobby because you get to write about what you love, whether it's money (what I mainly blog about), sports, fashion, celebrities, carpal tunnel syndrome, or worm farming. (Yes, there are plenty of blogs out there for the worm farming enthusiast.)

Blogging can be fun, but it can be so much more than that; it can be an extremely profitable business. That's what I wanted because in addition to doing something I loved, I also wanted the freedom, security, and financial stability to allow me to opt-out of my nine-to-five corporate gig.

So why wait to monetize your blog? There's really no reason. Later in the book, I'll cover the details of how to go about setting up ads on your blog. At this point, however, I want to stress the importance of setting them up early.

Some bloggers fear monetizing too early because they don't want to annoy their readers. They're afraid that a ten-second ad or popup on a free content site will irritate people so much that they'll stop visiting. That really doesn't happen these days. Maybe in the infancy of the internet and the blogging industry, people got so turned off by ads that they went elsewhere for content, but that's not the case anymore. People are used to ads now.

Of course, there are outliers in any category of life. Some people will absolutely detest ads, but you're not going to make money off of those people anyway. If they're going to leave your site for something as minor as the annoyance of ads, they weren't going to stick around anyway.

Sites like YouTube, Facebook, and Instagram, for example, have influenced people's acceptance of ads. People found enough value in using those sites that they were prepared to endure a ten-second ad. The key for those sites and any other, including yours, is to not overdo it.

As long as you're delivering value, sparing use of ads will not cost you any viewers. If you're producing complete nonsense, you won't have any viewers to worry about anyway. So, the point to remember here is to provide real value with your content and monetize right away, because the risk is low. A few ads spaced appropriately throughout your website aren't going to turn many viewers away. Not monetizing as soon as possible is just throwing all that ad revenue away.

DON'T STRESS ABOUT THE CONTENT TOO MUCH

Putting words online is not the path to profit. Rather, in the blogosphere, profit is all about attracting and retaining customers. The blog isn't necessarily the message; the blog is the business. Therefore, it helps to think of your readers as customers. That perspective will change your entire approach. It turns the main purpose of your blog into an avenue for reaching your clients, where you can satisfy an added opportunity to upsell them.

All too often, I encounter bloggers who don't understand that they're running a business, and like any other business, a big part of its success lies in its efficiencies. They fail to recognize that valuable content is just one part of the efficiency equation in a blogging business. They worry incessantly over the quality of the content, and that's not efficient at all. In fact, it's a surefire recipe for burnout, which is a surefire recipe for failure.

Nobody is going to bother with your blog more than once if all they find there is gibberish. However, it also doesn't do you any good to produce the most beautifully articulated professional prose on the internet. For instance, it doesn't matter that Robert Shiller, the Nobel Laureate Yale professor of economics who created the Shiller CAPE ratio, wrote the most brilliant research paper in the history of academia. That's great, but who is reading it? No offense to Professor Shiller, whom I have a great deal of admiration for, but a decent blog about something much less meaningful could attract just as many—if not, more—readers. Have you read his paper?

Think of the numbers. How many brilliant research papers could anybody possibly write in a year...one, maybe two, or three at the most? By contrast, you could write fifty or more ordinary blogs in a year that could attract a larger readership and make more money.

In the beginning, it might take a little longer for you to write content. Just don't stress about it. Eventually, you should be able to get your writing time down to about thirty minutes to write a blog of about 500-1,500 words. To keep your site fresh in the minds of your clients, you'll want to write about three of these per week.

If you find yourself with a case of writer's block, you're thinking about it too much. The best way to avoid that is to write what you know. As I said before, it could be about anything. If ants are your thing and you think nobody else cares about it, you're wrong. Don't believe me? Get on YouTube right now and type "Ant Channel" into the search bar. You'll find some channels have over a million-and-a-half subscribers.

In a world of over seven billion people, there is an audience somewhere for your passion about ants or anything else. In fact, in a niche market like that, you will face much less competition, which could translate to even more money for you.

The sweet spot is content good enough to provide value, but not so finely tuned that it keeps you up at night trying to brainstorm new ideas and exercising your creative genius.

FIND YOUR CUSTOMERS

Perhaps the most important takeaway from this chapter is that you need to be active in finding your customers. Whether you're Robert Shiller from Yale or Joe Schmo from Idaho, it won't matter if nobody knows you exist.

Nobody is going to try a new restaurant in town if they don't know it's open. So, budding restauranteurs hit the streets to introduce themselves and maybe put up a giant, "Grand Opening" banner on their storefront. They might even hire someone to wear a giant chicken costume and hand out flyers and samples of popcorn chicken. (My completely off-topic advice: beware of free food handed out by a menacingly cheerful six-foot-tall chicken on a street corner.)

Unfurl your own banner. Leverage Google AdWords or other online marketing sources. I'll discuss many of them in great detail later on, but for now, understand you need to let people know you're open for business. You can't make money in any industry—blogging, food service, or anything else—without customers, so get out, preach the value of your business, and find your customers.

STARTING OUT

When I started my blogging business, I was also still working my day job and multiple side hustles for about seventy to eighty hours per week. Blogging just happened to be one of those experiments I mentioned.

Fortunately, I still had time to take small breaks throughout the day. Everybody has at least a couple of small breaks in their work routine to get something done. Labor laws in most states actually dictate that everybody gets some sort of mandatory break, so I recommend maximizing the opportunity this free time presents.

Make the best use of whatever time you have for breaks in a day. I used mine to work on building my social media presence, which is a hugely crucial aspect of my turning-words-into-cash methodology. Use that time to "like" a gif or a post, leave a comment, or interact in any other way with your various social media accounts. The more you engage, the quicker you'll be able to grow your audience for your own blog.

Looking back to when I started out, I made one mistake that delayed my success by just a bit. I should have tackled social media and blogging at the same time. Instead, I invested most of my time early on into social media almost exclusively. Then, once I felt comfortable with the audience I had built on the various platforms, I focused on my blog.

You should be able to dedicate enough time to building your social media presence and anywhere from one to three blogs per week, even if you're working a full-time job in the beginning. If you can accomplish these tasks simultaneously, you'll be able to achieve success in half the time I did because I did them separately. That means you'll be able to leave that full-time job and reap the rewards of a passive-income lifestyle much more quickly than if you do only one at a time.

If you have only enough time to dedicate to one—either social media or blogging, I recommend focusing on the social media first, because that endeavor will build your readership base for when you do have the time to blog, later on.

HOW MANY SUBSCRIBERS DO I NEED?

Most social media users have 100-200 followers regardless of whether they have a blog. Whatever your base of social media followers, direct them all from your social media pages to your blog right away.

The blog is where you're going to generate revenue via ads, affiliate partners, and proprietary products. Chapters

Seven and Eight are going to discuss that in detail. At this moment, you just need to know that the more social media followers you have, the more people you can direct to your blog, which means more opportunities to generate income from those three sources. From there, you'll be able to implement multiple income streams, such as ads, affiliate partners, and proprietary products.

That's the whole business model, in a nutshell. It's not rocket science; it's not even eighth grade chemistry. It's simple math:

> *More social media followers equal more blog subscribers, which equals more income.*

There is no magic number of subscribers you need to own a successful blogging business. But the more you have, the more money you can make. In the next chapter, I'll talk about building social proof, which is a verification of your expertise, trust factor, and value as a blogger. To establish that, you need around 10,000 followers.

One important thing to remember is to not restrict yourself from any platform based on any personal disassociation. For example, Instagram is generally targeted at the eighteen to thirty-five-year-old age demographic. If you're fifty years old (Facebook's largest demographic), don't restrict your reach. Just because you think you can't relate to Instagram's demographic doesn't mean you still can't go after their user base. Nothing ventured means nothing gained, and you've got nothing to lose by reaching out.

HOW OFTEN DO I NEED TO POST?

You'll notice a consistent theme throughout this book is that I detest best practices. I like to go against the grain, and if I have an idea, I like to act upon it quickly. Because I like to move fast, I don't get hung up on an exact number for anything. I just do more of what does work. Therefore, I don't believe any magic number of posts guarantees success in your blog or on your social media, but I do follow some general rules that have worked quite well for me.

There is a happy medium when it comes to posting content. Too much looks like spam. People get suspicious that you're just posting non-stop repetitive, meaningless garbage. You definitely want to avoid that sort of reputation. Too few posts, however, has the opposite effect—people forget about you. Neither extreme is ideal. You've got to find the happy medium, which you can discover by testing for what works best.

If you have to choose between posting too infrequently or too often, go with too often. You'd rather be considered *spammy* than forgotten about. If you're viewed as spammy, people will just ignore you most of the time, but at least you're still relevant in their world, and once in a while, they'll probably check out something you have to say.

One of my mentors—Grant Cardone—is one of the spammiest people on the internet I've ever known, but he has a real estate portfolio that has a mind-bogglingly high value. I probably read about one out of every hundred emails he sends me, but that doesn't bother me.

Your particular industry niche is a factor in finding the right frequency as well. For instance, some influencers have meme pages that do amazingly well, but they need to post a new meme every ten minutes because that's what their audience wants. By contrast, an accounting blog would probably post once or twice per week.

If you're looking for a universal measuring stick of sorts regarding post frequency, I would start by posting or publishing something at least every day across all social media platforms. I would recommend one post per day in the beginning until you garner some legit social proof.

If you're running short on time, don't stress too much about what you're posting. Around 30 percent of your posts can be about anything at all. They don't necessarily need to be relevant to your blog or industry niche. These posts can be more related to who you are, what you like, and your sense of humor than anything else.

You want to make sure you're constantly relevant in people's minds at first. Once you get established, you can probably tone down the blog frequency. These days, I'm posting about three blogs per week, but I did much more in the beginning.

TIMING IS NOT EVERYTHING

Frequency is important because that's how people develop a relationship with you and your content. I place far less value on the timing of content, however. A lot of bloggers obsess over timing, always trying to find the best time to post something that will draw a huge readership. But honestly, I consider timing to be mostly irrelevant and advise you not to waste much time on it. Contrary to what you've heard so many times before, timing is not everything.

A lot of bloggers, especially in my niche, post on Monday morning. However, very few of them post anything on Saturday or Sunday. That's the unwritten, but universally accepted best practice of the blogosphere, but of course, you know what I think of best practices. Therefore, I challenge that go-to method of timing.

I understand that people want to unwind most weekends, so reading a blog may not be tops on their list of priorities during those days, but 500- to 1,000-word blogs take around ten minutes to read, so there's still time on Saturday and Sunday for most readers to enjoy their favorite blogs.

Viewers also get bombarded with new content on Mondays, and tend to read only their favorite content. So, why battle all the competition in such a saturated timeframe? Why not break away from best practice and try posting on a Saturday? If it doesn't work, you can always try reposting it on a Monday a week or two later, because there's nothing wrong with reposting content.

If you have the choice between competing or an easy-win...this is business, so go for the easy win. I don't like competition. Who needs it?

You never know when your blog is going to strike the reader at the right time. For example, if you post something with the title, "The Top Three Pizza Toppings You Have to Try" at 1:00 p.m. during the workweek, you might not get the attention of the people who just had lunch. However, if you post it at 5:00 p.m., right before dinnertime, when everybody is coming home from work exhausted and not in the mood to prepare an elaborate dinner, you might get a few more hits.

Once you have a decent following, you can repost content. If you post a blog that becomes a dud, readership-wise, try it again at a different time of the day, month, or year. Remember, you're not getting charged per post by anybody, so you may as well test everything you possibly can.

On Instagram Stories, you can display stories, have your readers swipe-up to your blog, and the posts will disappear twenty-four hours later. You can repost those in any combination and catch people at different times and moods to get views.

One catch with reposting is that the more familiar your readers are with you, the more they will tolerate your spam. A reader who doesn't know you is much more likely to stop following you. As your number of followers goes up, however, their tolerance goes up, and the more often you can repost content.

New posts will always generate more traffic anyway, so be sure to capitalize on that by saying something like, "New post! Check it out here!" Once your social proof is established and your followers trust you as an expert in your niche, you can mix in some recycled content very effectively.

What is the best time of day to post a blog? I recently attended a conference where wildly popular blogger, Neil

Patel, was speaking, and he said the best time of day to post content is 9:00 a.m. PT. This is typically when most people (on the West Coast) are arriving at their jobs and are ready to do a quick, comforting glance at some of their favorite topics.

Engagement takes a drastic dive until around 6:00 p.m. After that, most people start settling into their routines at home and might be looking to unwind with some online content again.

Analytics from my Instagram account align pretty well with Patel's recommendations, but it's not a huge difference. For instance, I might get only 80,000 sets of eyes on a post at 1:00 p.m., instead of 100,000 at 9:00 a.m., but posting at only certain times of day can be limiting, so I wouldn't be afraid to try any time of day.

Just remember, timing is not something you should be concerned with—don't waste your energy mistakenly thinking that timing is everything, because it doesn't really matter.

SETTING SPECIFIC GOALS

My goal is to make $100,000 per day from my blog. I like to aim high! That figure usually makes people either question if they heard me correctly, check my temperature, or call for a mental health counselor, but that is truly my goal. Actually, I might be a little too conservative with that figure, because there is no need to put restrictions on your earning potential. Blogging is like any other business; the more you put into it, the more you'll get out of it.

When you start out, you may want to set smaller, more-achievable goals, for some quick reassurance. For instance, think about trying to earn $100 per month from your blog to start with. After you achieve that, shoot for $1,000 per month; then, $10,000.

Approach monetary goals as if you're going up a staircase; take one step at a time. You might be able to leapfrog two-to-three steps occasionally, but if you miss, you could break your face, so it makes more sense to take incremental steps throughout your blogging journey.

After reading this chapter, you have a big-picture view of blogging as a business. You've established some expectations and gained some insight on the beginning of your entrepreneurial journey. Most importantly, you learned that there is almost no risk involved and a whole new world of profits and rewards to be gained. Take those words with you throughout the rest of these pages and into your blogging business.

In Chapter Two, I'm going to tell you all about how to

build that incredibly important social presence, which will be the fuel for your money-making blogging engine.

BUILDING SOCIAL PROOF

I feel pretty good about making over $900 while sleeping last night and over $30,000 per month in passive income, but that is circus peanuts compared to what Kylie Jenner recently accomplished.

Within the first eighteen months of launching a social media campaign, Kylie Jenner made over $420 million, according to CNBC. She will also be the first self-made female billionaire. Currently, she is making one million dollars per sponsored post on Instagram. I almost feel like an underachiever now.

That was the first time a product made so much money with a traditional marketing investment of zero dollars—

no commercials, no paper advertisements, no events, nothing else like it. Her vehicle for making hundreds of millions of dollars in such a short amount of time? Snapchat and Instagram.

This is proof positive that social media is the new capital in today's global marketplace. Think about it; if you have 100,000 followers on social media, how can you *not* make money? That means you're getting in front of 100,000 people.

It's easy to become desensitized to how massive of an audience 100,000 people is when you're used to seeing celebrities and other influencers with millions of followers.

To put 100,000 people in perspective, think of it in terms of a basketball arena full of rabid fans. Currently, the arena with the highest seating capacity in the NBA is The United Center in Chicago, Illinois, which holds just under 21,000 people. That means if you have 100,000 followers, you're able to get in front of five, sold-out basketball arenas every day, any time, and as often as you want, without paying a dime. You also have complete control over your advertisement.

For our purposes, consider social proof, which is an inherent cognitive bias of the human brain, to be the result of having a large mass of followers. Your first hundred or so followers will consist mostly of friends and family members.

From that foundation, your audience will then grow further by engaging with coworkers and followers you find elsewhere. This is the process of establishing social proof for blogging, which will grow the more you work at it.

You need to establish a base of social proof to successfully build your brand. For instance, it only makes sense that a person with 10,000 followers obviously has a bigger influence online—and therefore more social proof—than someone with only 1,000 followers.

To get a good grasp of how it works, consider if you were looking to follow someone to learn about an area of interest (fashion, movies, marine biology, etc.), wouldn't it be safe to say that you would be much more likely to follow someone with 100,000 followers than someone with only one hundred? That is social proof at work, because a number that big puts a few thoughts in everybody's minds:

- Why are so many people following this guy?
- He must have something of value!
- Maybe I should follow him too?

There's a reason why so many more people buy Nike

shoes and drink Coca-Cola products than other brands. It's because they see everybody else doing it. The brain needs to validate a lot of information in a short period of time when it's making purchasing decisions, so it uses pre-set inclinations based on what others are doing to save energy and time.

The key is to convince those first few people to try your sneakers, soda, or blog. Work hard to get those first followers and your audience will grow exponentially from there. The same cannot be said for a different strategy to build a blogger audience, which is known as search engine optimization (SEO).

SEARCH ENGINE *SUB*-OPTIMIZATION

Building an audience through SEO is like trying to build a contest-winning sand castle on the beach one grain of sand at a time. Great SEO takes years to build. It's the language of the early 2000s. Having said that, most of the big bloggers today are old school and get a high percentage of their views from SEO, but they've been working at it for over a decade now.

Achieving the top Google result for a keyword related to your blog will result in a ton of traffic. However, there's no way you're going to dethrone a big blogger who has been cranking away on SEO for over a decade now, to do it.

The good news is that using social media expedites that process and can quickly bridge the gap with these industry leaders in a fraction of the time it took them to build their audience. For example, my website, www.tubofcash.com, which is only about two years old as of the writing of this book, gets an average of 200,000 monthly views; approximately 5 percent of them come from search engines, while the other 95 percent comes from social media.

Audience growth is a numbers game that can be won with social media. When you're starting out, using SEO is going to take too long to overcome what is potentially the biggest obstacle to your success, which is obscurity.

HATING YOU IS BETTER THAN NOT KNOWING YOU

Suppose you're an aspiring restauranteur with a grand opening scheduled for today, but you've done nothing to get the word out that you exist. That wouldn't be a very good recipe (pardon the pun) for success. You could serve the best tapas, sushi, burgers, pizza, or any other food in the world, but your business would fail if nobody knows about it.

Obscurity is the biggest problem for any business. In fact, it's so big that you'd rather be hated than be obscure. Consider the case of Donald Trump. It's proof that if you can get half the country to really hate you, you have a standing chance to become President of the United States, not in spite of how polarizing you are, but because of it.

You certainly don't need to be polarizing either, but you do need to be recognizable in the mind of your audience.

STRANGER THINGS

You can't worry about everybody liking everything you do on social media, and you can't be afraid to network with random strangers either. Lots of people are. I get it, because I'm more on the introverted side of the personality spectrum, but you need to make sure people know who you are and where to find you.

Everyone is a stranger when they first meet. I go to a lot of networking events and see how comfortable people are with connecting to random strangers, as long as it's an in-person interaction. They shake hands, offer a polite introduction, and voila! They're instantly connected and no longer strangers. The same thing happens on social media, but some people don't see the correlation. (A lot of female bloggers are hesitant to follow strangers online, though it's not much different from connecting with someone they don't know at a networking event.)

For some reason, there's a misconception that meeting

strangers in person is okay, but doing it online is creepy. The only difference in these situations is the medium, but when you meet someone face-to-face, you may be meeting someone who shares none of your interests. However, on social media, it's very easy to see if you have something in common with someone.

GETTING TESTIMONIALS

Once you're comfortable meeting people you don't know, it's time to approach people for help in growing your business. Getting people to write testimonials for your blog is a great way to build social proof, and there is one incredibly simple way to do it—ask.

Suppose you have one hundred followers who keep engaging with your website. At that point, they're not just one-time curiosity seekers; they're repeat viewers. Approach four or five of those repeat viewers with a quick message, "Hey, I really appreciate you checking out my site, thanks! I would be super grateful if you could write a testimonial for me that tells others what you like about it. Hope to see you again soon!"

Some readers may even approach you first. If you have a place on your blog that accepts comments and feedback (and you should), they might leave you a few words of praise once in a while with something like, "Just wanted to say, I love your blog!" Those people are just about begging to be used as testimonials. They're low-hanging fruit, and all you need to do is ask. "Thanks so much for the kinds words. Do you mind if I use that as a testimonial?" Then, put their positive feedback close to the top of your page for all the readers to see.

As few as four or five testimonials will go a long way to establishing strong social proof. They act like Yelp reviews for your blog, and they really grab the eyes of newcomers, who will respond extremely well to a few words that back up the value of your blog. You can also use your landing page to display guest postings and other appearances you've made on television or radio.

If you can get a picture of the person providing the testimonial from their Instagram account, that will greatly increase the effectiveness of it. Make sure it's a picture of their face though, because it's crucial for your readers to be able to see that for the testimonial to have any real impact.

Testimonials are a great way to acquire social capital, which is more important than financial capital these days. If you have enough followers, you'll have no problem monetizing anyway. Financial capital can be burned through; it means almost nothing. Social capital, however, will make you money now and going forward.

TOOLS

Now that you understand some of the basics involved with building social proof, it's time to investigate some of the tools that can assist you even further.

Whether we like to admit it or not, businesses exist to make a profit and social media platforms want to make a profit just like any other business. Therefore, they provide some useful tools to attract other businesses to advertise on their platform. It only makes sense.

These advertisements generate a lot of revenue for social media platforms, but that doesn't mean that the sites ignore the individual customer. Without customers on the site, businesses won't want to advertise. Social media advertising tools offer a win-win solution for a wide range of stakeholders.

"SWIPE-UP"

The "swipe-up" feature, popular on platforms such as Instagram and Snapchat, is particularly beneficial to a blogger. Originally, they granted access to the feature for verified celebrity profiles only, but now they've also opened up to businesses and individuals. The feature allows users to swipe-up to go to whatever link the business designates.

There's a right way and a wrong way to use "swipe-up."

When executed correctly, bloggers can really capitalize on this functionality.

The wrong way (I should know because I've tried it) is to dryly post something like, "Go to Tubofcash.com." Almost nobody will respond to that because there is virtually zero enticement or incentive to click through. However, you're likely to get a lot of responses if you post something like, "Are you interested in knowing how I made $900 last night while sleeping? Swipe-up to find out how you can do it too!" See the difference mere language can make?

At the end of the day, using these features is all about the testing. Play around with language and other nuances to make the most of the feature. When you find something that works, keep doing it!

ANALYTICS

Another useful tool is analytics. Only businesses can use analytics, so make sure you classify at least one of your pages as a business page. Realistically, you should have a business and personal account for each platform, if possible. But, if you can choose only one, make sure it's a business page.

Analytics provide verification of whether or not your content is working for you. This is incredibly useful, because you can see the unique reach and impressions for each post. You can see how many people saved the post or liked the content. Facebook does this for its business profiles, and Google Analytics will do the same thing when you enter your website information.

The numbers provided by your analytics also show you the value of your business. If your analytics are good enough, your blog could become a valuable asset for another business to acquire. Plenty of bloggers have sold their blog for a lot of money; I know one, in particular, who sold for millions of dollars. The following paragraphs illustrate how something like this can happen.

One or two million dollars is a tiny drop in the bucket for a big financial institution to invest in acquisitions. Therefore, if you run a personal finance blog that already has an established user base with hundreds of thousands of monthly views, your blog would potentially be an extremely attractive investment for a big financial institution. Why? Because they would be able to display unlimited upsells and ads on your blog after the purchase.

Furthermore, your viewers already have an interest in personal finance, which makes them a "warm" audience. By "warm," I mean they already like the topic and likely have a higher propensity to purchase financial products and services than the average consumer.

I'm sure that scenario exists in most other industries as well, so the lesson is to not underestimate the lucrative potential of your blogging business. Of course, most blogs are not sold for millions of dollars, but a small percentage of them are, and there's no reason that you can't aspire to have one of the select few that is sold for a high profit.

SHOUT-OUTS

To develop a blog that's a valuable enough asset for someone to spend millions of dollars on, you're going to need all the help you can get. Actually, even if your goals are much more modest than that, why not get whatever assistance you can?

Shout-outs can be a great help from your colleagues to build your audience and it's totally free, so take advantage. They occur when you get praise from another blogger or influential figure. When that happens, you reap the rewards of his or her followers potentially checking out your blog, based on the recommendation from a person they're already following.

There is a classic "you scratch my back and I'll scratch yours" approach you should take with shout-outs. It's called, Shout-Out for Shout-Out (SFS), and it works simply by finding another blogger within your broad niche, giving them a shout-out, and asking for one in return.

You can always go for a bigger fish in the blogosphere sea, but you have to approach that a bit differently. There's a much smaller chance of getting a shout-out from someone with a much larger following than yours.

You need to sort of humbly approach them with a soft sell. Message them something like, "Hey, I'm a *huge* fan! I'm also just starting out a blog of my own. Would you mind helping me out big time by giving me a shout-out?"

This is really a Hail Mary attempt, and it will fall short about ninety-nine times out of a hundred, but what have you got to lose? Inevitably, there is going to be one big-time blogger who is in an especially good mood the day you approach them, and they will give you a shout-out. Remember, the other ninety-nine fails don't cost you anything, so it's worth it to go for this particular kind of Hail Mary shot.

I've sent more than a thousand DMs and emails, and inevitably someone says yes...eventually. My advice is to create a template and send emails, because the chance of your email getting noticed is much greater than it is via direct message.

Keep in mind, however, that there's a big difference between a Hail Mary, which will succeed around .01 percent of the time, and something that's just a ridiculous proposition. What I mean by that is, don't expect someone like Kim Kardashian or Oprah to give you a shout-out...ever. Instead, focus your Hail Mary efforts on people who aren't Instagram famous, but still have a healthy number of followers. One out of a hundred or so will probably help you out, as long as you have a decent page with nothing terribly offensive on it.

It doesn't take much to increase your reach. What happens if you shout-out one hundred people with 10,000 followers each and you get a 10 percent response rate? That's 100,000 more people you can reach for free! The simple math always seems to work in the tenacious blogger's favor.

Audience growth is exciting to watch! Imagine watching your number of followers grow from 300 to 500. Then, from 500 to 1,000 and so on, all the while realizing that with each new follower, you're getting more opportunities to convert them to more income. Acquiring followers is such a critical element to blogging success that one chapter isn't enough to cover it. The next chapter will dive into even more specifics about how to effectively use social media to grow your network.

CHAPTER THREE

GROW YOUR NETWORK

Your first priority as a blogging business owner is to establish social proof. Invest whatever time, effort, and even a little money (if necessary) to grow that initial user base. Eventually, that foundation will bloom to a large audience that views you as an authority on your chosen topic.

Some people are embarrassed to show their blog to anyone. Even the people closest to them. I think that's a mistake; it's part of a defeatist mindset that is not a good indicator of success. Public scrutiny is going to be part of your life as a blogger, so you might as well get used to it.

If you're uncomfortable sharing your blog with people you know, ask yourself if you'd rather have everybody in the world know about your blog or nobody. If your answer is nobody, then this isn't the business for you, because you value privacy over growth, which is fine, but it doesn't align well with turning words into cash.

You want *everyone* to know about your blog—family, friends, and random strangers. Don't let a distinction between your inner circle of close confidants and people you don't know become a roadblock to your success. Approach your blogging business with a positive mindset that is open to all seven billion people in the world, no matter who they are.

For some reason, people can struggle with this concept. Remember, your blog is a business, and if you were a business owner of a café, clothing store, or anything else, you would want everyone to know about it. Any business owner with the right mindset for success would want that, and so should you.

SOCIAL MEDIA IS EVERYTHING TO EVERYONE, EVERYWHERE

Here's a riddle:

What are two things that Baby Boomers and some Gen Xers might have that millennials and Gen Z never have?

The answer: *business cards and newspapers.*

People below thirty years of age are using social media for the functions that were formerly fulfilled by these two popular items. Sure, sites like *CNN* and *Fox News* are going to generate a lot of viewers looking for news, but the newsfeed on Facebook, tweets on Twitter, and informational posts on other social media sites are the chosen source for news-gathering among most millennials.

Business cards...really? Just...no! If someone asks you for a business card, resist the urge to say something like, "Sure, let me just look into the 1994 section of my wallet and pull one out for you. I think it's right next to the inserts with the wallet-sized photos of my friends and family I took with my Kodak Instamatic." Instead, ask them to look you up on Instagram (tell them, "Not to be confused with Instamatic") or any other social media site where you're looking to build an audience.

Once someone follows you on a site like Instagram, you can message them directly from the app to establish an immediate connection. Contrast that ease of use with the inefficiency of handing out business cards at meetings and industry conventions. Imagine 300 people handing each other a business card. At end of the day, they threw them all into the trash because who wants to carry 300 business cards around with them? Their wallets could only fit ten at the most.

The Yellow Pages and the PennySaver (coupon books) are two other business items from yesteryear that today's generations just don't bother with anymore.

If members of Gen Y and Gen Z don't know what a business card is, they sure as heck aren't going to know what the Yellow Pages are! Twenty-five years ago, if you needed the phone number for a plumber, an electrician, or another service provider, you would scramble to find the Yellow Pages in your house, flip through an alphabetized listing of companies, and call the number on your rotary-dial telephone. Today, you whip the smartphone out of your pocket and Yelp it...done deal.

The PennySaver or something like it, still manages to find its way into my physical mailbox from time-to-time, and it goes directly into the trash along with 99 percent of the rest of the snail mail I receive.

It's amazing how much money people still spend on direct mail, because it's a waste of money in today's social-media driven marketplace. The problem is that people get used to doing what they've always been doing. They forget to ask themselves, "Why am I spending $5,000 every month on direct mail if I'm getting close to zero ROI with it?"

Businesses want to get in front of people; that includes

entrepreneurs, freelancers, and independent contractors. Social media, on various platforms, offers a much more effective marketing tool than the Yellow Pages, business cards, or direct mail. The key is to know which platform will reach which generation.

DIFFERENT PLATFORMS SERVE DIFFERENT PURPOSES, BUT THEY'RE ALL WORTH YOUR TIME

Different platforms serve different demographics. Truthfully, you want to attract everyone you possibly can to your blog, so you'll want to get on all the platforms, but you should still know which platform will attract which user, so you have the ability to direct content accordingly.

FACEBOOK

We're going to touch more on the massive power of Facebook and how to effectively leverage it later in the book. If you decide to invest some money in your business, placing ads on Facebook is the best place to do it because their data allows you to execute your campaigns in a very scientific manner.

It's also important to keep in mind that Facebook's reach is nearly ubiquitous across all generations. Yes, Baby Boomers and Gen Xers make up the largest portion of Facebook users, but there are still a big portion of millennials and Gen Z users on the platform as well. More succinctly, Facebook is the biggest fish in the social media pond, so be sure to dedicate proper time and effort to this platform when trying to reach any generation.

Back in 2016, Facebook suffered some intensive media backlash and public scrutiny with their misappropriation of users' data that may have affected the presidential race. As a result, their stock dropped a whopping 16 percent in one day.

What's going to happen to Facebook next? I would predict that their business will suffer close to zero long-term consequences. Facebook might need to figure out additional regulations and restrictions. Maybe the laws will change around how data from social media sites can be used. In the long run, however, Facebook's momentary lapse of public support will be nothing but a tiny blip on the radar. They are the biggest fish in the pond with over two billion users across the globe. Whether or not they eventually make adjustments to appeal to people beyond that user base remains to be seen, but for now, they're not going anywhere.

TWITTER

Twitter is mostly a news source for Gen Xers, but a lot of other people are on it as well. There aren't many Gen Z users on the platform, but it's still an effective chatterbox among most generations to voice their opinions on subjects that are important to them, and they engage in current affairs.

Among my inner circle, I would estimate about one in every 400 people are on Twitter, so it's not a hugely impactful social media site for bloggers. It might not be worth focusing a huge effort on, but you don't want to ignore it.

Most traditional bloggers with a strong social media presence have a Twitter account, particularly my older millennial colleagues. This is a bit of a strange phenomenon, however, given its lack of significance among the readership of most blogs.

LINKEDIN

LinkedIn is a different animal than all the other social media platforms. Technically, it is a social media platform, but it's more like a business networking site where just about every professional with a desire to succeed has an account.

Despite this universal appeal to anyone who is serious about their career, LinkedIn still isn't very relevant for most bloggers. Blog posts don't get enough "likes" or "shares" to make it worthwhile to invest a significant portion of your time. I'm still on it, however, and I suggest you do the same, because you want to expand your social media presence to as many different platforms as possible.

Besides, you never know when things will change for a particular platform. One day, LinkedIn and Twitter could both make unforeseen changes that attract huge potential followers for bloggers. It's impossible to predict the changing social media landscape.

Here's another reason to never thumb your nose at a social media site, thinking it might not get you a lot of followers: A CNBC contributor recently contacted me after reading one of my blog posts from LinkedIn. She said she found my blog to be uniquely interesting and she wanted to interview me about it. I gave her the interview and they published it, which is super exciting to me, and none of it would have happened if I hadn't been on LinkedIn!

People almost never engage with my posts on LinkedIn. That's okay because every time I post something on LinkedIn, my Google Analytics shows me that at least twenty people go to my blog from it.

PINTEREST

A lot of people claim that Pinterest isn't really social media, but it's very popular in the blogosphere. The conversion rate on Pinterest from a monetization standpoint is actually higher than any other platform, so it's definitely worth your attention.

I can't say this with absolute certainty, but my theory on why the conversion from Pinterest is so high comes from the factors surrounding their biggest demographic. According to a lot of people in the personal finance blogging community, there are a lot of millennial, stay-at-home moms on the site. This demographic tends to be fairly affluent with a lot of disposable income, which of course leads to an easier conversion to monetization.

A good portion of Pinterest's largest demographic use the site to search for something like the top ten recipes for crockpot chicken. In fact, my wife (who, interestingly enough, is a registered nurse, not a stay-at-home mom) uses the site quite frequently as a recipe-sharing network.

Whether they're working moms or stay-at-home moms, many of the users get an image of something they like and tend to click-through to the blog. Likewise, if an ad pops up during their interaction, they have a tendency to click-through that as well. The ad might not be for a food pic either; it could be for a babyproof item, a pair of shoes, or something else that appeals to the reader. No matter what the ad is, it tends to stir the impulse to buy in the user or remind them that it was an item they wanted to buy previously.

SNAPCHAT

Without a doubt, this is the youngest demographic of all platforms. The vast majority of their users are presently under age twenty-five with a large percentage of them being under age eighteen.

Snapchat is 100 percent clickbait. There is no room for talk. The platform is built to make it like a new kind of TV, similar to YouTube and Instagram.

INSTAGRAM

Of all the social media platforms so far, I've received the most engagement and monetary conversion results from Instagram. From a sheer volume standpoint, the platform generates a ton of traffic for my brand. Instagram is considered the number one social media platform, with the biggest demographic being people aged eighteen to thirty-five years old. I suggest you develop as large a presence on Instagram as possible, based on the successful results I've received. Here are two things I've learned from that experience:

1. **Short-attention-span theater.** You have anywhere from three to ten seconds to get the typical Instagram user's attention. Their demographic isn't quite as young as Snapchat's, but it's still much younger than the users you'll find on Facebook or Twitter.

2. **Memes, memes, and more memes.** Memes work well on most platforms, but they're particularly effective on the picture-based Instagram. They get tagged, shared, and saved more than any other post, especially if they're relatable, so spend some time creating a steady influx of funny and relatable memes on Instagram, and you should get some positive results.

This section provided just a sampling of some of the most relevant platforms available. The key is to not thumb your nose at any of them, because social media is always changing. Just because some platforms reign as all-powerful today, doesn't mean it will stay that way forever.

I WILL FOLLOW...YOU SHOULD TOO

Non-bloggers don't usually understand the value of spending a few hours or more per day liking, commenting, and direct messaging with people online. The reality is that those people you engage with will eventually translate into dollars.

A fairly large percentage of people I follow, follow me

back. That may not be the case for you in the beginning because you don't have that social proof yet. However, the law of reciprocation can work very much in your favor when you are established. If you doubt that conclusion, break it down to simple math.

Suppose you follow about 400 new people per hour across different platforms. That equates to about 6,400 per day, assuming we only count our waking hours. If only 2 percent of them follow you back, that's still 128 new followers per day. There's no better way to build a customer base for any business, without spending significant money.

Customer acquisition typically costs anywhere from $5 to $100 per customer, depending on the target audience and industry. If you're a real estate investor looking for leads, you might spend over $100 per lead. For a blogger, however, customer acquisition via social media can be comparatively inexpensive. Better than that, if you follow someone and they follow you back, that's free.

Of course, each platform has different algorithms built in to prevent people from just spamming everybody on the site with comments, posts, or ads. These preventative methods are constantly changing, so testing is the only way to know what the limit is. What's acceptable one day might not be the next, and you could get blocked, so you need to be careful. It might be okay to follow 110 new people today, but a platform may decrease the number to ninety-eight tomorrow.

I tell all my club members to follow the maximum number of people. Today, the maximum number is 7,500 on Instagram, 5,000 on Facebook, and unlimited on Twitter, but who knows what those numbers will be tomorrow? The key takeaway is to not be afraid to follow 7,000 new people and only get seventy who follow you back. Whatever you get back is still worth it because there's no associated acquisition cost, other than your time.

LOOK FOR NICHE INFLUENCERS

Although you want every human you can possibly reach to know you and follow you on social media, you still want to know where your largest following comes from. A large number of followers is great, but followers who are actually interested in reading your blog are much more ideal because they are more likely to engage, purchase, and remain customers.

To more specifically target your followers from your industry niche, you need to find an influencer, which is someone with a big industry presence or a celebrity who is widely recognizable. If you're trying to perfect that blog about worm farming, go find a celebrity worm farmer.

Okay, that might not exist, but you can still find whomever it is that is the leading authority in worm farming.

Once you locate that predominant authority, check out their social media pages and see who is following them. Then, try to get those same followers to your blog. One important thing to keep in mind, however, is that anywhere from 15-50 percent of all influencers or celebrity followers are bogus, because they're bots.

BEWARE OF THE BOTS

Most of the big social media names like Oprah, Kylie Jenner, and many others admit that up to 50 percent of most influencers are fake.

Understanding that you could be wasting your time following a bot, I wouldn't just follow people from an influencer's social media profile at random. One safeguard against that is to start by only following people who comment on the influencer's page. Those are the highest quality leads because not only are they proven to not be bots, but they're also likely to engage.

Bots aren't the only danger to beware of in the social media marketplace. As with any endeavor that has the potential to make a lot of money, there are a lot of shenanigans happening in the background of the blogosphere as well. Most people aren't talking much about it, but you can't be naïve to it, because this isn't just your hobby anymore; it's your business.

BOOSTING

Another tactic to beware of is boosting. Some platforms—like Instagram—prioritize posts with comments attached to them. Therefore, a lot of influencers have employees or hired groups to comment on their posts, to seem more influential and trick the algorithms in an attempt to get their post to appear at the top of search results.

Bots and boosting are going to happen. The rules and algorithms these platforms put in place are constantly changing, but so are the tactics, so you need to adapt to whatever occurs in the entire ecosystem. Just remember, getting social media followers is still free, so you might follow one hundred people in an hour, and fifty of them might turn out to be bots, but who cares? You still acquired fifty new followers!

GROWTH BRINGS MORE GROWTH AND SO ON

All of the things I'm explaining in this chapter are important for growth, but perhaps the best way to grow is organically through word-of-mouth recommendations.

It's only natural that once you get a certain number of followers, a percentage of them will like what they read on your blog. It's likely that a certain percentage of those people will then tell others what they liked so much. People might tag you on social media with a comment that says, "This is what I was telling you about the other day." Your user base can grow substantially from that kind of positive word-of-mouth advertisement.

For instance, if I have 200,000 followers and someone sees me on the Explore page of their Instagram or through a topic I hashtag like #money, #blog, or #bitcoin, they might check out my page. If they like what they see, they might tell their friends and followers, "Hey, this is pretty cool. This guy really knows his stuff." From there, I might get a whole new group of followers.

MAKE YOUR JOB EASY

Growth is crucial to the success of any business, but a blogger's growth can be seriously stunted if you stress out too much about your content. It's difficult—at best—to concentrate on how to grow and make money, if you're overwhelmed with what to write about next.

Keep in mind that sometimes people exhaust the topics they want to write about because they've narrowed their chosen blog material too specifically. I urge you to beware of this trap and accept my recommendation for avoiding it, as follows.

Suppose you blog about the Golden State Warriors, but you've written everything there is to write about them, from Steph Curry's favorite food to the color of Draymond Green's dorm room at Michigan State. If that's the case, it's time to broaden your horizons. Maybe you should start writing about the NBA in general, college basketball, or other sports.

You should ensure there's enough flexibility within your chosen niche to change subjects with a fair amount of regularity. This speaks to something I'll elaborate more on in Chapter Five, which I call writing to the broad niche. If you have five synergistic subjects, you'll never have writer's block.

Synergy in your overall business methodology, among topics, platforms, and everything else, will be a key to your success. In the next chapter, I'll discuss a little more about how to create this synergistic vibe to your brand.

CHAPTER FOUR

CREATE SYNERGY

Synergy is important because it helps your audience identify with who you are. If you do it right, you can even blog about multiple areas of personal interest. One way to do that is just by staying true to yourself. If you blog about what you know, you can create a synergy among three seemingly unrelated topics.

Whatever you write about though, make sure you keep it real. Don't blog about worm farming if you don't know some serious stuff about worm farming. However, if you know about worm farming, baseball cards, and underwater dancing, feel free to blog about all three. The synergy will create itself because you are the common denominator that ties all three together.

KEEP IT REAL

I'm a big believer in keeping it real. If you do that, creating synergy among all your various social media accounts is easy. There are no fake realities, alternate personas, or anything else to remember to keep up with. Any time you post a comment or blog about something, if you're keeping it real, there's no worry about saying something contradictory on a different platform.

Being yourself and blogging about what interests you will also contribute to sustainability, which is perhaps the most important factor in writing content for a blogging business. The reason that sustainability is so important is that most people can succeed in most ventures, as long as they stick with it, and writing content that you actually enjoy will go a long way in helping you stick with your blog.

I've noticed the biggest obstacle to anyone being successful in their blog is boredom. If you're not writing about something that you're truly passionate about, your blog could fall victim to boredom, which means that writing content will become a chore for you, progress will inevitably slow down, and so will your desire to keep the blog running.

However, if you're writing about something you're deeply invested in or genuinely passionate about, the content won't become a chore and you'll have a much better chance of sustained success.

KEEP THE HATERS IN PROPER PERSPECTIVE

Occasionally, I post pics of my child and Bible verses, and I almost always get someone who says, "Dude, I'm following you for advice about bitcoin, not this BS." To which I respond, "Bye!" For every follower that shuns me for those things I hold near and dear to my heart, another new follower engages because they liked the content as much as the other person was offended by it.

Yes, I get a lot of backlash for my Christian and conservative views from non-Christians and people who lean on the liberal side of politics. Do I care? Not as much as you might think, because even though half the population might hate those opinions, the other half might align really well with them.

This attitude of not taking the haters too seriously isn't just a nonchalant or irresponsible mindset either. It's more about being realistic, because if someone stops following you for a reason as silly as posting a Bible verse or a pic of your child, they were going to unfollow for some other reason at some point anyway, so don't sweat it.

Although I try to keep the haters in proper perspective,

it still affects me. I'm not a robot, but I don't dwell on it either, and that's how I suggest you handle the haters as well. Preach the truth to yourself and the negativity of others won't seem overwhelming to you.

I don't recommend engaging with the haters, but one time I direct messaged someone back who left a particularly nasty comment on one of my blogs. Instead of getting involved with some sort of verbal sparring match, however, I decided to just ask them, "Dude, I'm sorry you feel that way, but is there anything I can help you with?" The response I got back was, "I'm sorry man. I was having a really bad day and I took it out on you. My bad."

Believe it or not, most people don't have enough free time to troll the internet and espouse their vitriol on your blog. If they lash out at you, it's probably because they were just having a tough time and your blog merely gave them the opportunity to unload with a high degree of anonymity.

You don't need to be liked by everybody, because if you try to be Switzerland (neutral) all the time, you won't get either side. Nobody will hate you, but you also won't be worth anybody's time. Keep it real and you'll be better off for it in the long run.

For instance, it's easy to post nothing but positive things on your social media pages, but it's not realistic. Unfortunately, this tends to be a popular practice. People love to post on Facebook when their children land the leading role in a school play or donate their allowance to charity, but they're much more reluctant to post about when their kids get caught smoking cigarettes in the restroom at school or spray-painting the town library with graffiti.

When you're using social media as a core component of a business blog, however, you should post the good with the bad. You don't need to post about anything you're not comfortable with others seeing, but when you post nothing but positive developments over and over again, you become unrelatable.

RELATABILITY

Relatability is the strongest marketing strategy available. You need to effectively use it to establish your brand.

For a good example of how relatability works, consider the contrast between two popular Hollywood actresses—Jennifer Lawrence and Gwyneth Paltrow. Lawrence is universally loved because she's a bit goofy and has a good sense of humor. She seems "down to earth," which makes her relatable. Paltrow, on the other hand, seems aloof, unapproachable, and not at all relatable.

MMA fighter, Conor McGregor is a good example of relatability in action as well. He throws money around and acts flashy, but his status of an underdog makes him likable and ultimately, relatable. He seems like just another guy who made it to the big time, and people love that. They can really get onboard with someone who seems "just like them," no matter how brashly he talks or acts.

As a blogger, it's advantageous for you to seem relatable as well. You want your viewers to see your brand as something they can identify with, not something they want to avoid, can't understand, or is out of their reach.

FACE TIME

As a blogger, your face is your brand. Fancy logos and gimmicky banners are fun, but it's your face that people will associate with your brand and therefore, relate to. People don't relate to animation or graphics, but faces are very relatable. You want to put your face on your business and blog profiles so that people can see it whenever they read your content. It's your commercial, your brand.

Other businesses pay big money for commercials that don't have a big ROI on them because it keeps their brand relevant in the consumers' minds. Bloggers need to implement that same tactic. I write some posts purely to keep the image of my brand fresh in the minds of my followers.

SOCIAL MEDIA'S BEST FRIEND

Make sure your readers know they're following a human being, not a robot. Placing your face on your profiles will be key to establishing that, but so will posting relatable content. Share things that are a big part of your life, so your viewers can feel more connected to you.

The more you consciously audit your audience to see what they like and dislike about you, the more draining it will be for you to continue blogging. You'll risk burnout and unsustainability at that pace. Instead, simply blog about what makes you...you. The rest will take care of itself.

One of the most relatable things in the world is a dog. People who have pets—particularly dogs—love posting pictures of them, and they love viewing other people's pictures of their dogs as well. Is there anything more universally amusing than the picture a dog tearing open a misplaced bag of beef jerky or getting into some other form of trouble? So, if you have a dog, post some good dog pics and memes. Do the same thing for baseball, food, fashion, or whatever it is that you enjoy most out of life.

Keep it real, so don't get a dog just to post pictures, but if you have one and you're a dog lover, it's a "liking" and "sharing" goldmine, at least in the US. That's not the case all over the world, but American culture and some other areas of the world are very pet-friendly.

(Of course, some people take their pets a little too seriously. For instance, I know somebody who is leaving their entire inheritance to their dog. Of course, this assumes that the dog will outlive them, which is not the most likely of scenarios. I'm not even sure of the legalities involved with such a position, but that dog could have one sweet collection of chew toys someday.)

The more you know about how people work and what they like, the more relatable your content will be and the greater the chance of getting followed is. Pets are just one part of it. People like to know they're not alone. They want to feel comforted by the idea that other people experience the same likes/dislikes, wants/needs, and positives/negatives that they do.

EVERYBODY LOVES A MEME

Nobody loves a mime, but everybody loves a good meme. Mimes are weird and annoying, but memes, on the other hand, are funny and relatable.

A truly effective meme has the ability to make someone laugh and think, "Oh my God, me too!" It could also remind them fondly of a friend, in which case they may tag them and say, "Dude, this is *soooo* you!"

Recently, I put a lot of memes on my page; some of them

didn't even have anything to do with finance, but they were hilarious. One particularly funny meme I posted was from a Zach Galifianakis movie where it shows him doing math in his brain. I added the caption, "This is every millennial trying to figure out how their friends afford their lifestyle." It's current, ironic, and downright funny, so it was quite popular.

It's okay to break away slightly from the air of professionalism sometimes to share a laugh with your followers. This is acceptable for almost any business, but it's especially welcome in a blogging business where you're not sitting in a stuffy boardroom talking about stock prices or pounding the pavement while stressing about finding qualified sales leads.

SYNERGY WITH OTHER BLOGGERS

Based on the three billion internet-connected people in the world, the blogosphere has plenty of love to go around, so don't be afraid to share your audience. Your blog isn't some sort of literary cult where readers are forbidden to go beyond a figurative zone of your influence.

People come to your blog because they find some value—functional or personal—in what you have to say. The more you try to control what they see and don't see, the more followers you will lose to other, less possessive and controlling bloggers. Why try to control something you have no control over anyway, especially when you can be an integral part of the process?

I try to create a synergy with other bloggers in my broad niche by including relevant links to their blogs in my own content, and I recommend you do the same. There's an inherent value associated with linking similar content to your blog. It strengthens the relevancy of your content. Essentially, your blog becomes the "go-to" place where people start their exploration of related content. This establishes you as a leading authority within your broad niche.

There's also the law of reciprocation to consider when you're linking to similar blogs. If you refer people to other resources, I recommend reaching out to the other blogger and telling them, "Good stuff here. I thought my audience would benefit from it, so I included a link to it. Check it out." Hopefully, that plants the seed for them to reciprocate and give you a similar shout-out at some point. If they don't get the hint right away, you can always circle back a week or two later and say, "Hey, I just posted something your readers might like. Would you mind linking to it? Thanks!" You've already given them some free readers, so the least they can do is return the favor.

You'll also get the perks of SEO from a backlink, which is

when a link to your content appears on someone else's blog. Google takes both inbound and outbound links into account in their search results. Although we're not paying any serious attention to SEO rankings because it takes too long, we're still happy to take whatever bump in keyword searches we can get.

There's another benefit to creating synergy with other bloggers as well, which is guest posting.

GUEST POSTING

Early in my blogging career, I used to ask to guest post on other people's blogs. About a hundred bloggers said no, but two accepted my offer and they both had tremendous followings. I guest posted on two blogs: www.retireby40. org and www.budgetsaresexy.com. The results were unbelievably successful in both cases.

All I had to do was reach out to those bloggers and say, "I'm also a blogger in your niche. I just created a blog post that I think your readers might respond well to." This might seem like a time-consuming activity, but it's not if you craft an email template that you can send to all the bloggers in your niche. It might take you thirty minutes to do that and it's well worth your time.

As a blogger in the beginning of your career, you're not

likely to get quite that outstanding of a response, but even if the approach gets you 1,000 views, that's still something you can build from.

Those bloggers who let me guest post on their website prepared their audience for my input. They said, "Today, I've got a guest from www.tubofcash.com, and he's got a cool blog I think you should check out. Here it is."

Sure, 98 percent of the bloggers I approached said no, but all I needed was one or two to say yes. If I needed three or four to say yes, then I might have emailed two-hundred bloggers. Like so many other aspects of a blogging business, it comes down to simple math.

Don't be afraid of collaboration with like-minded industry professionals. Not everyone is going to be willing to share, so be prepared to get rejected by 98 percent of the people you approach.

To turn the odds of acceptance slightly higher in your favor, try approaching people with a similar, but not exact, match to your niche. For instance, if you're a makeup blogger, reach out to a fashion blogger. They'll be more willing to collaborate because they don't view you as a direct competitor. Compose an email template that says, "Hey there! I'm a makeup blogger with a lot of readers who like fashion too. I'm sure your audience is looking for makeup tips, so maybe we should work together?" Doesn't that sound like an extremely reasonable and mutually beneficial business proposition? Of course it does.

Know your audience, be relatable to them, keep it real, and create synergistic content across all your platforms. If you can accomplish that, you'll have a tremendously good chance to run a highly profitable and successful blogging business.

In the next chapter, I'm going to explain all about how to write to the *broad* niche. This is an important concept that walks hand-in-hand with creating synergy.

CHAPTER FIVE

WRITE TO THE *BROAD* NICHE

In my undergrad school days, my professors used to always talk about the customer avatar. That approach is so dated. I'm not selling to avatars; I'm selling to human beings.

Most bloggers cater to a small group of people within a particular area of interest, but that's too granular. It makes more sense to serve a broad niche with synergistic topics. In other words, a fashion blogger could easily write about makeup and all aspects of fashion. Writing exclusively about just shoes, handbags, or accessories would be too limiting in scope.

Although there is a specific group of people who are

already knowledgeable in money, most people around the world are still interested in the general topic. Best practice, which I am generally opposed to, would dictate that I write exclusively for that narrower audience of people with some financial expertise. However, I see that equally as limiting as the previous fashion example, which is why I choose to write with the broader niche in mind instead.

The content will naturally carry over to the smaller group with some preexisting knowledge, because it aligns well with their principal interests. More importantly, however, it will especially benefit the more general audience, who otherwise wouldn't have known how to make money through stocks, cryptocurrency, or whatever the subject matter of the day is.

Ideally, it's nice to appeal to multiple audiences within the same broad category of topics. For example, my blogs about Bitcoin probably aren't going to attract a lot of attention from the people looking for information about worm farming. That would be too far removed from my general category of personal finance. My most frequently posted topics—cryptocurrency, stocks, and generalized personal finance have synergy.

When I write a blog about the general topic of cryptocurrency, chances are that it will attract some readers who are interested in developing technologies, such as blockchain. Also, the blog may attract other readers who aren't necessarily interested in cryptocurrency, but are followers of real estate, because they're both financial instruments as well.

My content theory is to never get pigeonholed into one narrow subject matter. In other words, it's fine for me to write about worm farming a few times if it makes me happy.

Actually, I suggest writing about random topics in around 30 percent of your blogs because it keeps things interesting for your reader and it provides some insight into your personality. It also makes the content creation far less monotonous, both to create and to read.

KEEP IT ORGANIZED

If you have more than one topic you blog about, you need to make sure your content is well organized and easily navigated by the user. For example, if you're writing about worm farming, dance fighting, and formula racing, make sure each target audience knows where to go to find their relevant content. You don't want your dance fighting readers to have to sift through worm farming content to get to where they want to go.

You should have an easily identifiable "Menu" bar at the

top of your homepage that clearly separates each topic area for your readers. Think of the webpage for a news site, where the top navigation area has different news subjects—Sports, Entertainment, Weather, etc. Readers can click the area that interests them the most, and bookmark it for future reference.

Within each category, you want to have your biggest stories at the top. Again, it helps to think of your blog like it's an online news site where the most current and important stories are at the top of the page.

Good organization of information on your website adds to the user experience. If the user finds valuable content and they don't get frustrated with your website's usability, you're more than halfway to managing a successful blog.

WHAT SHOULD YOU WRITE ABOUT?

Creativity for me is a pretty random process. Miscellaneous thoughts cross my mind constantly, and I'd wager that you're not much different in that regard. If one of those random thoughts seems like it might be a good idea for a blog, I suggest writing it down immediately. Keep your notes app open and ready on your phone or tablet, so you can quickly jot down information like this when it comes to you.

By writing down ideas or even actual titles for blogs throughout the day, you'll pretty much eliminate writer's block. By contrast, you'll go from facing writer's block to wondering which of an overwhelming choice of blog topics you should cover. Right now, I have around 500 different ideas, titles, and rough drafts for blogs ready for me to expound upon whenever the time is right.

HOBBIES

Start thinking about what interests you. Money, fitness, career, and business interest me, so that's why I write about those things. You might be a hardcore gamer or a rabid sports fan. Maybe you're a fashion expert, movie buff, or purveyor of fine soaps. The possibilities are limitless for material. All you need to do is choose the topic(s) you are most interested in and start writing.

If you're having a hard time figuring out what you're truly passionate about, look for social cues from your family and friends. Do people often tell you, "Dude, you are *always* talking about videogames." If that's the case, you're a gamer! Start writing or vlogging (video blogging) about *World of Warcraft*, *Madden*, *Grand Theft Auto*, or whichever game it is that you currently like the most. When you've exhausted the content in that game, move on to another one. Then, maybe branch out into different consoles, e-sports competitions, etc.

QUESTIONS AND ANSWERS

Once you've selected your broad niche of topics, you might still occasionally get stuck thinking of what to write about. If that's the case, start thinking about what kind of questions your readers, as well as friends and family, are asking you. As an authority figure in a topic, you'll get questions from others seeking expertise.

So far, I've only posted a few blogs about cryptocurrency, but I'm getting a lot of messages asking me questions about it.

"Hey, when is Ethereum going to rise up again?"

"What's your view on Ripple (XRP) in the next three months?"

"How impactful do you see bitcoin becoming over the next five years?"

These are prompts for potential blog posts. Sometimes we overthink our problems and don't see the answer when it's right in front of us.

This method can also use the comments section of your blog. If a reader leaves a question like this, your writer's block could be solved simply by providing an answer to the commenter's question in the form of a blog post, rather than a quick two to three sentence response to the individual questioner.

You can start a new blog by saying something like, "I've been getting a lot of questions about this lately, so let me just share my thoughts with all of you here." Then, elaborate on the subject matter in the body of your blog. See how easy this is!

CHECK IT OUT

Another way to inspire blog ideas is by a quick Google search. Think about what your readers would likely search for, and Google it. Notice what comes up as the number one search result. Is it more than a year or two old? Are they an old school blogger whose numbers are going down? Are you trending in a positive direction as a blogger? If the answer is yes to all those questions, you can use that to your advantage by creating your own blog related to that topic.

The next thing you should do is leave a comment on that blog, asking the creator for an interview. From there, you can collaborate to reproduce the blog from a different angle. Of course, not everyone will be willing to do an interview with you, but you have nothing to lose by asking.

Sometimes people get really weird about protecting their

blog. They think if they work with you they'll lose their audience and not be able to recoup it. As if sharing a readership is a bad thing; it's not! In fact, it can usually work to both of your advantages. Some people just have a very finite way of thinking, and that's okay because that's not the way you'll think. By reading this book, you'll understand how many pieces of the blogging pie there really are.

A PIE WITH THREE BILLION PIECES

The planet Earth is currently home to 7.6 billion people. According to research done by Google, three billion of them have internet access through 2020. One blogger cannot possibly reach all three billion people (although you can certainly try). Even if you did reach all of them, those people are all likely to have more than one interest anyway. So, if they're looking at me for information on money and fitness, they can still look to your blog for sports, fashion, food, or countless other topics. The point is that there is a virtually limitless number of pieces to the blogging pie.

THE SKY IS *NOT* THE LIMIT

There is no limit to the amount of money you can make, and whatever you earn shouldn't affect the income of other bloggers. Money is not scarce, though we think it is.

One analogy I like to use is that people used to get paid

with salt. They thought it was scarce. That's where the saying "worth your salt" comes from. In fact, there was a time when salt was so valuable, people would kill each other for it. These days, you can get salt anywhere. It's available for a small price at the grocery store, or if you ask your neighbor nicely, they'll give you some for nothing in return.

Unfortunately, some people look at money today like people used to look at salt in much earlier days. They think it's scarce, but it's not. Even salt was limited in its quantity, but money isn't limited at all. If you make $100, it doesn't mean that someone else can't. There's enough money in the world for everybody to grow their business.

The sky is not the limit with your financial growth through blogging, because there is no limit.

WORD COUNT

There's a fine line between a blog post that's too short to have any real value and one that's so long it bores your readers. You want to find a word count range that hits the mark for your particular audience. Having said that, if you stick to a specific length—no matter what the content dictates—you risk getting stuck in some best-practices vortex and the whole experience will become a chore.

A lot of bloggers will say your blog needs to be at least 1,500 words, but I've never found that to be true. In fact, when I try to force a minimum word count, not only do I get frustrated, but the content seems so forced and ineffective that the blog loses value.

Start out by creating short, snappy posts because your blog's early adopters will come from social media where they're used to getting a quick snippet of information. Make it even more palatable for them by breaking up the blog into bullet points, numbered lists, and short paragraphs.

After you've hooked your audience, you can produce longer blogs and tell them upfront that the subject matter may be a little more complex than some of your previous posts. Even suggest that they bookmark or save it for later, because there's a lot of valuable information in there that they're going to want further access to.

GIVE YOUR READERS WHAT THEY WANT

Without a doubt, the most important part of any blog is the title. You need to come up with an attention-grabbing title. If the reader isn't at least intrigued by the title, you have no chance; they're not going to read your blog. After that, the first two to three sentences are also critical. If the reader isn't hooked after this, you've still lost them.

Okay, if you're such a master wordsmith that the reader has actually read your title and the initial two to three sentences and they still want to keep reading, congratulations. They might actually read the rest of your blog, or not.

At the first sign of rambling, keyword stuffing, or nonsense of any kind, your reader will swipe, click, or do whatever they need to skip the rest of your blog and move on to the next thing. Truthfully, even if they are interested in what the title and introductory sentences have given them, they might still only skim the rest of it.

With the collective shorter attention span of everybody today, I usually provide a TLDR—too long, didn't read—summary at the end of every post. I sum up the key points of the blog in bullet points of two to three sentences each. One strange thing about that is that a lot of people who find something interesting in one of those bullet points will scroll back up to the main body of the blog and look for more detailed information. If it's a platform like Instagram Stories, I might have them swipe-up to see more related content. Then I can earn some money from the ad views.

Most readers are looking at blogs because they want takeaways. They want to be able to read about a few quick and dirty tips that will help them accomplish a task or learn more about a topic. It's a good idea to remember that blog readers like to scan for sections of content. They don't normally read one long flowing piece of text from start to finish. Remember, your readers aren't looking for Shakespearean prose. They want to get what they came for and get out.

Congratulations! If you've made it this far, you've already learned a lot about how to create a successful blog and are well on your way to financial freedom. I've still got some good information to share, so keep moving forward into the next chapter, which will explain some of the key elements to a landing page and how to convert random visitors into loyal subscribers.

CHAPTER SIX

VALUE-ADDED CLICKBAIT

By now, you know all about the importance of building a large presence on social media and some tips and tricks for creating a decent blog, but you might be wondering how to bring those two worlds together. How do you get people to click on the link in your social media post to get to your blog?

The answer is less about content and more about design of your landing page than most people think. In fact, around 94 percent of people linked their trust of a website to the design, not the content. (Elizabeth Sillence, 2004.)

Clickthrough rates make or break you as a blogger. Your success is dependent on whether or not you can get your followers to actually click through and read the blog. Content can't help you there. It can help people to come back, but it can't inspire people to make that initial commitment to read the first time. That's where design comes in, and it starts with clickbait.

ISN'T CLICKBAIT A BAD THING?

The word *clickbait* has become synonymous with disingenuous and unscrupulous business behavior over the years. It leaves a bad taste in people's mouths, kind of like anchovies for some people. When most people think of clickbait, they think they're going to get something completely different than what they thought they were getting when they clicked.

Clickbait remains one of the best ways to lose your audience. When poorly executed, it will damage any established trust and eventually, you'll lose everything from it.

Just like anything else in the world, however, there is a right way to use clickbait and a wrong way. After reading this, you're going to know the right way.

As a blogger, you need some form of clickbait to get people to click through to your blog. The best way to accomplish that is by writing a title that is enticing enough for people to give the content a chance.

Consumers are constantly bombarded with information and advertisements competing for their attention and the small window of free time they have. Therefore, your title needs to declare the potential for significant value in the article, and the content that follows needs to deliver on that promise.

Curiosity is also a big factor. If you can inspire it, curiosity is a powerful enough emotion—on its own—to get people to click through. I'm sure you've spent time browsing videos on YouTube before, and the way the title was worded, you became so overwhelmingly curious that you couldn't help but click through and watch the video to get on with your life. That's a real phenomenon. You know it's clickbait, but you need to click through just to get it over with anyway. It's happened to all of us.

My recommendation is to save your energy on the actual content, but invest more time in choosing the right title, because that's what is going to build your initial audience. Brainstorm titles, refine them, and make them as attention-grabbing as possible without lying. It's an art and a science, but it's not as difficult as it sounds.

HOW TO WRITE A CLICKTHROUGH-WORTHY TITLE

There are many ways to write an effective title, but perhaps the best one is to address and remove a particular pain point for the reader.

One of the most common aspects of humanity is to avoid pain. Whether it's physical or emotional pain, we generally don't like it and want to know how to eliminate it or avoid it as much as possible.

If you have a fitness blog, you might try a title like, "Do You Want Six-Pack Abs?" or "Do you Want to Lose Twenty Pounds?" There's a big problem with those titles, however. Readers already know they can accomplish both of those goals, but they also know it's going to involve some pain. They're going to need to do a million crunches or eat nothing but kale salads and quinoa crunch bars for a year-and-a-half to accomplish anything.

What if, however, your title read something like, "Do You Want Six-Pack Abs? Here's How to Get It in Less Than Thirty Days!" You could even take it a little further with "Here's How to Get It without Ever Going to the Gym!" Those titles address and remove the reader's pain point.

Be careful, however, because you don't want to misrepresent anything. If you can't deliver on your promise, that might damage your reader's trust in your information, so you can't say something like, "Here's How to Get It while Eating Nothing but Doughnuts, Deep-Fried Bacon, and Beer!"

I tell people I'm a blogger and I make silly money doing it, so one of my titles is, "Do You Want to Make Money Blogging? Here's How to Do It with No Risk." The first part of the title gets people to buy in. They say, "Heck yeah, I want to make money blogging." The second part of the title removes the pain point from their false belief that they'll need substantial capital to get their blog up and running.

Nothing about what I said in those titles is a lie. I have a partnership with Bluehost and I tell my readers whoever uses my link gets a thirty-day money-back guarantee, along with a 60 percent discount on hosting. I say, "What is the worst thing that can happen in this scenario? You lose zero dollars and you're right back where you started, but at least you tried and won't wonder 'what if?' any longer."

USING IMAGES

Don't just slap on a title or flimsy call to action (CTA). Also, think carefully about the images you insert, because effective visuals can be powerfully appealing and convincing to your readers. In fact, it's a good idea to invest more time and effort, proportionately, in creating a solid title and choosing memorable images than writing the body of the content.

Don't forget that lesson, because it will be a strong determining factor in the success of your blog. The stronger your image, the more people will take action, because a good image will evoke an emotional response and people—as much as most deny it—buy based on emotion.

By now, you might be thinking that content is mostly irrelevant, but that's not the case. I'm just saying that it's extremely crucial to have an effective title and image to even give your content a chance.

A popular theory is that content is king, but really, it's the title and images that are king. Otherwise, everybody would have read Noble Laureate Professor at Yale Robert Schiller's theory on cyclically adjusted price earnings (CAPE) ratio.

You should integrate images into your blog wherever you can. Instagram doesn't allow links from your main-feed posts, but you can take a screenshot of your post, edit it, and put it on your feed with the clickthrough-worthy title on the top of it. If you attach a link to your blog in your bio from your social media platforms, people can click that to get to your blog as well.

Just remember that the more steps people have to take, the less likely they are to engage. That's the biggest reason I like Instagram Stories and Snapchat the most. There's only one step for your target audience to go through. They either tap on the bottom of the image or swipe-up to go to your link. That makes it incredibly easy for those users to discover how awesome your content is, which means it will be incredibly easy for you to monetize your posts!

Meanwhile, Facebook, Twitter, and LinkedIn automatically insert a hyperlink that brings up an image from the post, so users can go directly to that post. On the surface, this appears like the best of all worlds, but those three sites should only combine for about 5 percent of your total traffic as a blogger, who is primarily leveraging social media to grow your audience. Their users just aren't as likely to click through to read your content. Despite the fact that it's the quickest way to get to your content, you still can't expect a lot of traffic from them unless you pay for ads.

Posting pictures of yourself can be an effective way to engage people, as long as the image is relatable. Sure, people dream of being more than what they are, but it's hard for them to relate to you if you're standing next to a $140,000 Tesla. So, after you become a millionaire from reading this book, remember that!

If you want to show people how far you've come, try

sharing an image consisting of two halves; one that has a "before" image of you standing next to your beat-up, old Toyota Corolla, and another that has you standing next to your brand-new, expensive luxury sports car. This is similar to the Conor McGregor example of relatability. An image like this one doesn't come off as braggadocios in any way, and it doesn't inspire any negative emotions like jealousy or outright hatred either, because it lets people see that someone just like them has made it, and they can too!

You could come off as a silver-spoon-fed, trust fund type of story if you only post a picture of where you are today, without anything that accurately represents where you came from and the early struggles you had. People love the underdog story because they envision themselves in a similar situation; it makes you more relatable. People want to cheer for you, rather than envy you.

CLEAR FOR LANDING

The average person in the year 2000 had an attention span of twelve seconds. In 2018, that has dissipated to a mere eight seconds, which is a full one second shorter than that of a goldfish. Those are pretty telling statistics of our society.

Most people lose their minds if they have to wait for a

browser to load for more than a second-and-a-half in this high-speed internet connected world. Therefore, the landing page of your website better load quickly, and it better be equally as good at telling the user where they are and how to get where they want to go.

Gen Z and a large portion of Gen Y doesn't know what life is like without smartphones, so you need to understand that three-second window on Snapchat when crafting your content. Therefore, your landing page needs to be primarily mobile friendly.

Desktop applications are going the way of the dinosaur. In fact, some social media apps—like Snapchat and certain functions of Instagram—aren't even available for desktop or laptop browsers. Therefore, mobile design is a big priority for you, as a blogger. Sometimes, I have a design that looks a little wonky on the desktop but it looks perfect on mobile, and I go with it because I know that fewer than 5 percent of my readers are using a desktop to view my page.

ABOVE THE FOLD: GOD SPACE

The first thing people see on your landing page is known as "Above the Fold" by some or "God Space" by others. It's the most important space on your website and will determine your bounce rate, which is defined by Google as "the percentage of visitors to a particular website who navigate away from the site after viewing only one page." The better your god space, the lower your bounce rate, and the higher your viewer retention.

For two great examples of maximizing the impact of god space, check out Apple.com and Netflix.com. Apple accomplishes great design by providing nothing more than their logo and a slideshow of one of their newest products. It's beautifully minimalistic and effective.

Good design isn't what most people think it is. A lot of people approach web design like it's a serious expression of their artistic integrity or meant to be a showcase of their graphic design mastery; it's not, or it shouldn't be anyway.

Simplicity and functionality are what make for good design and the best overall user experience. Skip the fancy fonts and flashy animation. Instead, make good use of white space to accentuate the image or text you want your user to focus on the most.

The proper use of the god space on your website is crucial to having great design, so don't clutter it to show off how smart you are. Place an important image or content there, surround it with white space, and leave it alone. Your readers will love you for it!

DUMB IT DOWN

Your readers will also love you for keeping the content readable and engaging. A somewhat sad and alarming statistic is that the average reading level in the US is somewhere around seventh or eighth grade. It gets worse. According to a 2014 study done by Andrew Powell Morse, who researched 225 songs that spent three or more weeks atop *Billboard's* pop, country, rock, and hip-hop charts, the average song is at the third-grade reading level and the average number-one single is between a second- and third-grade level.

The moral of this story is that there's no reason to post doctorate level content if your audience is more interested in reading something they could find in the library of a public elementary school.

You might be perfectly capable of posting professional prose worthy of an intense scrutiny from some of the most scholarly book clubs across America, but for the sake of your blog, you might need to dumb it down a little. Avoid using overly prodigious wording that's brimming with academic sophistication. More simply stated, don't use big words when you don't have to. Get it?!

You also don't want to get bogged down with grammatical perfection. In a blog, it's okay to put a few exclamation points where they don't belong!!! The content should be much more conversational than professional.

Many of my newer friends are always correcting my blogs. They don't understand that it's okay to use slang and simplified common language in a blog. People don't want to pull up Dictionary.com in a separate browser when they're reading my blog. Rather, they want to get the information they came for and get on with their day.

My intention isn't to make sure my content meets the standards of the literary department at Harvard University. As long as my content is readable, engaging, and valuable, my time is better spent growing my business. So, I usually tell those people, "You don't get it then. Nobody talks like that. People don't have a conversation that ensures grammatic correctness at every level. I'm starting a conversation on my blog; not shooting for a Pulitzer Prize."

A lot of bloggers who are excellent writers and take pride in their ability to wordsmith content have a hard time with this approach. They don't want to lower their intellectual standards, but I'll tell them, "Look, is it more important for you to be right or rich?"

The simple truth is that most people can't relate to an English professor, but they can relate to valuable, engaging content, which is what you should strive for with your blog.

GETTING SUBSCRIBERS

Ideally, you want subscribers to your blog. It's nice to catch the occasional passerby and hope they come back to read your content with fair regularity, but what you really want is people who are committed to your content through subscriptions.

Like it or not, subscriptions require people to fill out a form. Keep in mind that most people hate forms, so keep your form as simple as possible. Have a name and an email field, but nothing more than that. Multiple boxes are a turnoff for most people and your chances of them subscribing go down appreciably with each extra field you force them to fill out.

I use popups to get subscriptions. You're probably thinking, "Popups? I hate popups! Everybody hates popups! Why would you do that?" As counterintuitive as it may seem, popups actually make the subscription process much easier on the viewer for a couple reasons.

First, blogs put their "Subscribe Here" field in random places. It's hard to find. The field could be on the top, bottom, left, or right. Nobody knows where to find it.

A popup will pop up in the middle of the screen, so the viewer doesn't even need to look for it.

The second reason a popup is better than a permanent "Subscribe Here" field is because the popup is saved in cookies and goes away, unless the viewer deletes their cookies. Therefore, I'm only annoying the viewer once with a popup, but a more traditional "Subscribe Here" field annoys the visitor every time they come to the page.

My form says two things; first I ask, "Do you want to learn how to make passive income?" This is similar to how I recommend structuring titles. I make the initial statement enticing, but I also anticipate the objection. So, I then add, "Get free articles and other useful resources!" Then, I provide an image, which is currently a guy sipping a martini with money pouring all over him. But I also anticipate the probable objection that I'm trying to sell something to the reader.

The actual form doesn't look like much. It has just the name and email fields, and instead of saying, "Sign Up" or "Subscribe Here," it says, "Count Me In!" because people don't like to subscribe or sign up for things. The more casual phrasing of "Count Me In!" however, seems less formal and more appealing, like they're opting in to receive free stuff and knowledge as in some sort of membership.

Subscribers are important in another way too. Businesses will pay big money for email lists. Therefore, your list of subscribers can become a big asset. If a company wants to buy your blog for an obscene amount of money in the future, your email list of subscribers will be a big part of what makes it happen.

UNSUBSCRIBERS: LET THEM GO

I believe so strongly in the value of my blog that I actually feel bad for the people who unsubscribe. Those people aren't going to have access to all that great content again. I don't, however, feel like I'm being rejected in any way.

People saying no to your blog is nothing personal. They're not rejecting you as a human being. For whatever reason, those people just don't want to engage with your business anymore, and that's okay because there's another three million prospects out there to make up for the loss.

When people ask me about unsubscribers, I tell them just to let them go. It's not worth your time and effort to try to save them. Don't get caught in a back-and-forth email exchange with someone who doesn't want to do business with you any longer and doesn't appreciate the value of your content. It's a bad idea to get involved in that sort of meaningless confrontation, because it could cost you a lot of valuable time and lost productivity.

Remember, you're providing a service with your blog. Believe strongly in the value of that service and feel confident in your ability to run a viable business that can lead to financial independence.

In the next chapter, I'll explain how to generate income from ads and affiliation sales. Furthermore, I'm going to show you how to make the most of these methods and more. Keep reading because now we're getting to the real dollars and sense of blogging for business!

CHAPTER SEVEN

CREATE INCOME STREAMS WITH AD NETWORKS AND AFFILIATE MARKETING

Let's say you've followed my instructions on building a social media presence; you've hit 1,000 subscribers to your blog...now what?

It's time to make some real money, and there are two ways to do that with your blog—ad networks and affiliations; both of these can be quite lucrative for the dedicated blogger.

AD NETWORKS

The first place to look when setting up an advertising network is Google AdSense, because it's free and you don't need a minimum number of viewers. Other networks feature higher payouts, but they require an already healthy viewership.

Mediavine and Adthrive each require at least 100,000 views per month, and most bloggers can't reach that number. You can't just lie to those networks either. They require permission to directly access your Google Analytics so they can have an unfiltered view of your traffic. Furthermore, you need to keep them connected throughout the duration of the partnership. Maybe someday you'll be able to partner with one of these networks, but until you're established, it's best to go with Google AdSense.

Once you set up the ad network, they do all the work for you. I have ads on every one of my posts, but I don't physically place any of them. I have a widget for the ad and a plugin on the backend that automatically does it whenever I post something.

Readers don't need to click the ad, sign up for the service, or buy any product for you to receive income. The ad network pays you for every 1,000 page views (referred to as revenue per thousand impressions or RPM), regardless of reader interaction. Therefore, every post you create becomes an income stream, as long as people are reading the content.

From there, you just sit back and enjoy the passive recurring income. Don't forget, those ads don't just generate money for a week or two. They earn income forever. As long as people are reading the blog, you earn money. It's that simple!

A lot of people can get discouraged early because they don't have enough readers right away. But once you establish a large enough reader base, you'll start to see the real value of ad networks. This is actually perhaps the biggest struggle for new bloggers to come to terms with, but I urge you to not give up.

Remember, your content never goes away. So, even if very few people are reading your blogs now; one, two, three, or more years later—when you do have a larger established reader base—those people will read the blogs you created years ago in addition to the current pieces. Furthermore, you'll still generate the income from that readership.

The moral of the story is, don't get discouraged if you're posting a lot of content early on that isn't reaching a lot of people, because years later, when you do have a bigger readership base, those same posts are going to earn more money. So, posting is never a waste of time.

The true beauty of working with ad networks is the huge number of big-time advertisers that are in them. These networks tally millions of views every month and that's a really powerful statistic to leverage in the marketplace.

It is extremely difficult for a blogger (especially a new one) to ask a Fortune 500 company to partner with them on their own. But, Mediavine and the other networks tell Honda, Apple, and other huge corporations that they can get them in front of 100,000,000 viewers every month, so it's a win-win for everybody. The advertiser gets the attention they want and the blogger gets the revenue they need.

CHEATING THE SYSTEM = BANNED FOREVER

Whenever a system is put in place, people will try to cheat it. It's a quirk of human nature to try to break through any established boundary and discover what happens once we do. In most cases, I say *Bravo!* to the individual who pushes the boundaries and doesn't take no for an answer, as long as it's legal and ethical. In this case, however, I say don't try it.

It's natural to start thinking of ways to break the barriers presented by ad networks, like Google AdSense or Mediavine. One thought that might occur to you could be to have friends and family clicking on your ads non-stop to get better analytics. Then, you might wonder if you can run down to the local Walmart, login to their display computers and click on your own sites a bazillion times to drive your numbers up. That's not something I made up. I've actually heard of people doing that. People will go to extraordinary lengths to try to beat the system, but you can't.

The algorithms designed by Google, Amazon, and others are way beyond whatever sort of amateur system hack you, I, or any other blogger in the universe can come up with. Even after saying that, you still might be tempted to say to yourself, "Well, what's the penalty if I get caught cheating? I'll probably get a warning first, and after that, I'll just have to behave." Wrong! You will not get a warning. Instead, you will be banned. Some advertisers, like Google, will ban you for life. If that happens, you're done before you even got started. Relax and play by the rules, because it's not necessary to cheat to make a lot of money anyway.

So, don't get greedy. Don't pull shenanigans. Just play it straight and the money will follow. There's no need to do anything else.

IT'S OKAY TO USE ADS

The old stigma of "selling out" by using ads to pay for your message is gone. People don't care if you use ads to generate revenue for your TV show, podcast, YouTube channel, blog, or anything else anymore. Ads have become a way of life today. We're completely desensitized to them, so get over yourself. Put the ads on your blog, because in the technological age, your readers understand they need to be there.

Ads will not soil your brand. However, if a small percentage of followers leave because they can't put up with the ads, guess what? That's okay. Let them go. If they were so intolerant that they couldn't put up with an ad or two on your blog, they would have left for another idiotic reason at some point anyway. *CNBC*, *The New York Times*, and *HuffPost* all produce content that is supported by ads. If those mega companies need ads to support their service, doesn't it sound reasonable that you need them too? Of course it does and almost everybody in the world knows it by now.

AFFILIATE MARKETING

Partnering as an affiliate is a great way to make a lot of money from your blog. How much money can you make? Anywhere from zero to millions of dollars. Your revenue depends on several variables including niche, specific partnership, and your following, among other things.

Suppose you're a prepper, which (in case you don't know)

according to Dictionary.com is "a person who believes a catastrophic disaster or emergency is likely to occur in the future and makes active preparations for it, typically by stockpiling food, ammunition, and other supplies."

As a prepper, your blog regularly features product reviews for various survivalist supplies like knives, rations, first aid, tools, and more. You could sign up for the Amazon Associates affiliates program, which would be a great niche-independent choice because everybody knows Amazon, and sales conversions are very simple.

AMAZON ASSOCIATES

By signing up with Amazon Associates, you receive a commission every time someone uses your custom link to purchase a product. Each product category has different commission percentages. The highest I've seen—as of this writing—is around 10 percent. However, Amazon has been steadily lowering commissions rates for some time now.

Even if someone puts a product in their cart, logs off, and purchases the product later from a different browser, you still get the commission as long as the transaction takes place within ninety days. Also, Amazon uses a universal cookie, which means you'll get commission on anything else that's put in the cart within twenty-four hours of your link being clicked.

It's fairly common for approximately 50 percent of your revenue from Amazon Associates to be from products that are never mentioned on your blog. As people browse Amazon from your link, they end up purchasing something else as an impulse buy, which happens more often than most people realize.

You don't need any intense web design skills or advanced marketing degrees to make this work. All you need to do is get a partnership with a program that sells products related to your broad niche. When in doubt, use Amazon, because of their universal appeal and popularity.

CLICKBANK

ClickBank is another reputable affiliate partnership you could do business with. Commissions will vary with any of them depending on the product and category, but shop around and you'll find one that suits your business best.

There is one big benefit to having ClickBank as an affiliate partner, which is that their cookies last much longer than Amazon's. Their commissions are also a little higher for a lot of products. Think of them as having cookies on steroids. The downside, however, is that their reputation is not nearly as strong as Amazon's.

Most people I know already have their credit card info

and billing address stored in Amazon. In fact, a lot of them have a Prime membership as well. Therefore, the odds of someone making a purchase on Amazon is much greater than them typing in their info all over again, and purchasing something from a random website.

BLUEHOST

My chosen affiliate partner, however, is Bluehost. I have a proprietary service with my private membership club for aspiring bloggers that creates a synergy with Bluehost, because every time someone signs up for my club, they're going to require hosting.

I discovered Bluehost by asking other bloggers in my broad niche who they used. Many of them made a lot of money with Bluehost, so I figured it would also work well for me. I filled out a quick form on their website and someone contacted me shortly after. It's been a partnership that has been wonderfully lucrative for me ever since.

My suggestion is for you to follow the same steps I did when searching for an affiliate partner. Ask other successful bloggers in your niche who they're using, and that should lead you to the pot of gold at the end of the blogosphere's rainbow.

In the beginning, it might be difficult for you to partner

with a dedicated affiliate program, because some of them want verifiable proof that you can sufficiently convert their links to sales. However, once you have a decent amount of traffic, you'll be able to partner with almost any affiliate you desire.

You don't need a ton of views to make an affiliate partnership work either. For example, if 1,000 people see you as an authority in your niche, then it's fair to assume that twenty of them are likely to make a purchase based on your review of a certain product or service. At that point, you can decide if you want to branch out into more products and services because you can see the rate of return working for you. The more you offer and the more you post, the more money you make. You don't need a Kylie Jenner-like viewership.

Blogging is not a one-dimensional income stream. You might need to retool your mindset to think of blogging as endless streams of income. You can use ads, affiliate programs, and create proprietary products, among other possibilities. The next chapter dives into the exponential earnings that are possible with proprietary products.

CHAPTER EIGHT

EXPONENTIAL EARNINGS

At this point, how to make money with blogging should be a little clearer. You have an understanding for how ads and affiliate partnerships can provide two steady passive income streams.

Of course, there are some things you need to do first. You need to establish a presence on multiple social media platforms, gain a following, and acquire social proof through your expertise in your broad niche.

What if you don't have time for those things?

What if you can't wait to get 30,000 views per month to qualify for a certain ad network or affiliate partner?

What if you want to make money *now?*

In that case, you can look into proprietary products and services as an income stream. Certain services can be implemented very quickly and they can be quite profitable as well.

Keep in mind, my recommendation is to execute ad networks and affiliate marketing before offering proprietary services, unless for some reason you have to make money as soon as possible.

Offering a proprietary product or service can make you money immediately, but there's a lot more work involved than there is with ad networks and affiliate marketing, because those products and services are already established. Meanwhile, you have to do everything yourself with a proprietary product or service because it's your own creation. It's a great way to make money fast, but it's going to be a little more labor intensive.

EARN MONEY *NOW* AS A SOCIAL MEDIA AGENCY

Out of all the proprietary products or services that I've seen people create, becoming a social media agency is the most lucrative choice; nothing else comes remotely close.

Consider that a restaurant's typical customer might net

them $10 per month, due to overhead and other expenses diminishing the overall profit. Comparatively, you can make thousands per customer as a social media agency.

A lot of people dream of opening a restaurant, which is a proprietary product. It's probably the number one thing people of all generations want to do, but it involves exponentially more work for far less profit than creating your own social media agency.

The businesses you target in this situation aren't quite big enough to dedicate their own employees to handle their social media pages, but they're not so small that they don't have enough cash to outsource it to you.

Most of today's small business owners are Baby Boomers (and some Gen Xers) who worked for twenty or so years in the corporate world and wanted to get the heck away from their boss and the rest of the rat race.

Generally speaking, these folks are not very social media savvy. They probably have a Facebook page, a LinkedIn profile and maybe a Twitter account, but they almost definitely don't have an Instagram, Snapchat, or anything else.

Those people may not understand the power of social media to drive revenue and increase profits for their business. That's where you can come in and create a win-win situation for both of you. You can leverage your knowledge of various social media platforms to increase their brand awareness for a reasonable fee.

A lot of business owners will pay anywhere from $500-$2,000 per month to have someone manage their social media for them. Maybe you're not comfortable calling yourself a social media expert or a professional marketer. If so, you're probably not giving yourself enough credit. If you know how to set up an Instagram account, you're already ahead of the average business owner.

Even if these business owners know how to manage their accounts, they can't do everything themselves. They have employees for a reason, so hiring you as an independent contractor to handle it completely takes that task off their plate. That alone could be worth the investment.

Keep in mind that these business owners aren't necessarily looking for the most highly qualified person to do this either. They just want someone who can do the job without their constant involvement, and it's worth it to them to pay a little to get it.

Set clear and accurate expectations if you're approaching someone about managing their social media presence. Don't overpromise anything. Instead, tell them, "Okay, I can maintain your existing Facebook account and set up an Instagram and Snapchat profile for your business as well. I will also post at least one thing every day." As long as you're capable of doing that, you're not overpromising anything.

Some of these businesses may not even have a website, or it could be a really poorly designed one. If that's the case, offer to set that up or update it as well. Not sure you're capable of that? Remember, it's incredibly easy to use WordPress to set up and maintain almost any website for any industry, because there's a free template for everything there.

Understand that 99 percent of small businesses, including restaurants, retailers, and others, have absolute abominations for websites. The free templates available on WordPress are much better than whatever blank canvases these people use for their website design. Trust me; whatever you can do through WordPress will be an improvement.

If a recurring monthly fee is too much for them, offer them a one-time fee for a one-time service of updating their website to a more modern appeal. You can always pull up the website of a competitor who has a superior website, and show them how they're losing business to them. That one update could help grow their business immediately, and it may encourage them to use you for future services.

Also, everything you could ever possibly need to troubleshoot is only a quick Google search away. Certainly, there are numerous YouTube videos available to help you with almost anything you need.

If you think about it, paying someone only $1,000 per month ($12,000 annually) to manage social media and direct marketing (email blasts to existing customers) is a steal compared to paying a full-time employee around $40,000 to $80,000 per year with benefits to do the same thing.

That's a powerful point to leverage when approaching a business owner with your proposal. Tell them, "Look, I'm going to take total control of this and you can focus more deeply on what you do best in your business. You don't need to spend crazy money on this. I can do it for much less."

If you can manage the social media for two, three, or more businesses, you'll realize a nice recurring income, and from a cash-flow standpoint, recurring income is awesome because it's more dependable than bonus chunks of money coming in, which is also great in its own way.

Don't underestimate your value in this proposal. You're winning by earning a fair fee in exchange for a valuable service. Meanwhile, the business owner is also winning because they're getting increased business from your expertise. What I said earlier about obscurity being the kiss of death for a business applies here as well, because social media is the key to letting people know that a business exists. The better you can sell that fact to business owners, the easier it will be for you to land as many clients as you want.

If you can acquire 1,000 social media followers (and you definitely can), you can help them take their business to the next level. That's another thousand people they can promote their brand to and possibly earn a long-lasting relationship with.

PROVIDE PROFITABLE PROPRIETARY PRODUCTS

Try saying that heading three times fast! Ebooks, courses, membership clubs, and physical products are all fabulous ways to add an additional revenue stream and exponentially increase your earnings.

Think carefully before you choose a product to offer on your website. For instance, clothing is usually a not-so-great choice, unless you have a million followers and a powerful personal brand. However, as long as you're seen as an authority in your niche, a lot of people will buy your book or e-course.

E-COURSES

E-courses are the easiest proprietary product to set up and monetize. If you're already blogging, just create additional content that features more detailed insight. Refer to the content as premium and make it strictly available to members who pay a monthly or one-time fee to access it.

Not sure how profitable an e-course can be? A mentor of mine created an online program seven to eight years ago. It took him about two days to create the entire series of content. The last time I checked on him, he had around 200,000 people paying him roughly $70 per month for the program. No need to do the math in your head because I'll do it for you. That's $14,000,000 per month for two days of work! Try earning that with a brick-and-mortar small business. I recently hung out with him at his $20+ million pad in Beverly Hills, so the proof is in the pudding.

On a smaller scale, someone else under the same mentor created an online Excel program that allowed them to earn low six figures, which enabled them to leave their day job. Strangely enough, all the information contained in that Excel program could be found online for free. A well-known phenomenon exists where a lot of people innately put value on anything that costs something and assume anything that's free is of sub-par quality. Keep in mind that by you creating the program, it's not a hodgepodge of information. You're providing value by curating the content, rather than them having to piecemeal all the information from separate sources on their own time.

Take the content a step further, if you'd like, and create YouTube videos. Create ten videos of thirty minutes each that offer premium content. Don't price the course too low because then people will assume it has little or no value. Suppose you price it at $2,000 for the entire video series. Of course, you shouldn't price it too high either, but if you have 1,000 followers and only twenty people (2 percent conversion rate) buy the course, that's $40,000 income from one course.

That sort of venture is fairly "set and forget," other than the marketing required to mention it on your social media from time to time. Why, you ask? Because the bulk of the work is in creating the videos. Once they're uploaded, you don't need to do anything else, unless you want to make it an ongoing online program. Otherwise, you can continue to reap the rewards of those videos for as long as people are purchasing them.

MEMBERSHIP GROUPS

The second easiest proprietary product to set up and monetize is a membership group, such as mine, which I call the Elite Bloggers Guild.

Human beings are social creatures. People especially like to connect with other like-minded individuals, so if you're passionate about woodworking, you want to hang out with people who know how to build an awesome fireplace mantle, porch rocker, or birdhouse. It doesn't matter if it's woodworking, sports history, or civil war trivia, people are willing to pay for a club membership that makes them feel like part of a select community.

Within ninety days of creating my club, 500 subscribers signed up to pay monthly dues for membership. I mostly act as a moderator for the club and the members talk to each other to increase their own knowledge base. Other than that, I do one live video stream per month where I share some sort of pertinent blogging information. I have members from all over the world, so I keep it unscheduled, but it's enough to keep my members in the know.

Another thing I do is offer a thirty-day money-back guarantee. I think that's extremely important because it lets your subscribers know that there's no risk involved. Most people don't leave, but it provides people with a valuable peace of mind when they sign up, so I recommend you do the same.

To attract club subscribers, I recommend having Design-Crowd or a similar service create a logo to put on your website or private Facebook group. This enhances brand awareness. Add a payment gateway via a simple plugin like MemberPress and you'll be able to receive money from your subscribers easily.

A lot of people overthink these things and attempt to create their own online forum from scratch. But, Facebook is already a very robust platform for creating and maintaining a private group. Most people are also already signed up through Facebook, so there's no need to create any login or anything else.

My club that currently has 500 subscribers on it, paying me $80 per month, which amounts to $40,000 per month, is through Facebook. I didn't create any special online forum. It took me about two days to set it up. I had DesignCrowd design the logo, but then I just slapped that on my Facebook private group and didn't need to think about setting up anything else.

I'm not affiliated with MemberPress in any way, but I use it as a dynamic and simple payment plugin that creates subscriptions and one-time payments. This is another example of how easy it is to make money blogging. A lot of people overthink this as well, assuming they need to create some elaborate payment structure on their website, but they don't. All you need to do is install a simple plug-in.

MemberPress even provides pricing templates that can be

woven into different membership levels. For example, my club currently has monthly payment options consisting of an $80 basic plan, a $120 VIP plan, and a $199 diamond plan. MemberPress allows the subscriber to click any option and be taken directly to PayPal or a credit card payment option.

When I created my club, a lot of people thanked me for creating such a value. It just goes to show how you shouldn't underestimate the value of your own content and services. A scarcity mindset exists where a lot of people assume that just because they're not willing to pay for something, that others are the same way. But, there are plenty of people out there who are willing to pay money for a gym membership and other clubs like an elite blogger's membership.

I used Facebook to create my club membership because they have "closed" or "secret" groups that can be set up in five minutes. You can also get creative with your club. I created a short video intro because I think videos are very powerful ways of getting a message across. Even if you don't embrace being on camera, you should do at least one video because people like to see a human being behind the service. They need someone to identify with, and you are the best ambassador for your own product or service to do that.

ABANDON ALL SELF-DOUBT

Don't let self-doubt creep in when creating premium content. You might think to yourself, "Who's going to buy this?" or "I have no idea how to create an e-course," but this model works. Sites like the *Wall Street Journal* and many others have been separating content this way for years. Some of them give you a glimpse of the article you want (a paragraph or two) and then provide an option to access the premium content by signing up for a subscription. A simple WordPress plugin will do that easily for you, too, if you want to go that way.

A lot of people overcomplicate the idea of selling proprietary products and services. They allow their heads to be filled with "what-ifs" and other forms of self-doubt, but you need to transform that to a confidence mindset that understands the value of your brand.

For some reason, people wait too long to monetize, waiting for that ever-elusive perfect moment. If you have no method of payment in place, however, nobody can pay you for anything, so why wait to install such a simple plugin? Without a product to sell and a payment method in place, you can't pick the low-hanging fruit from the monetization tree.

TOO EASY

Today's technology almost makes things too easy. There's a simple plugin to do almost anything a blogger needs to do. Gone are the days when you needed an expert programmer to design and build websites. Therefore, don't be afraid to experiment with proprietary products and services that can be enabled with simple plugins and add-ons.

Chapter Nine is a detailed look about how to spend money in blogging to make more of it. You don't need to buy ads to be successful, but it's an option worth considering to grow your business, and there are more ways than one to keep money coming in anyway.

CHAPTER NINE

KEEP THE MONEY COMING IN

When I was five years old living in Korea, I would ask my grandparents to take me to the countryside so I could catch tadpoles and frogs in the ponds and streams. It was a nice break from living in the capital city of Seoul for me. Afterwards, I would take whatever I caught and put them in freshly washed bottles with holes punched out of the cap, so they could breathe. Then, I would sell them to the other kids in the neighborhood. At the time, I probably couldn't have spelled the word *entrepreneur* in Korean, English, or any other language, but that's what I was.

If you're reading this book, you might have a similar

memory from your childhood. Maybe you don't, but you still know there's money to be made in the blogosphere. Either way, it's time to think of yourself as an entrepreneur now and start blogging.

A lot of entrepreneurs recommend a "pay yourself first" mentality, but you need to go beyond that if you want to continue to grow your business. Sustained growth requires putting some money back into the business and finding creative ways to generate more revenue.

SPENDING MONEY

I know a couple bloggers who don't put any money into their business, and one of them makes around $100,000 and the other makes around $300,000 per year, which are nice incomes. You might even be thinking, "Tim, I'm making $30,000 per year working the graveyard shift at the local 7-Eleven. If you can get me to $100,000 without having to leave my couch or invest any money, sign me up!" Okay, that's a totally valid response, and if it's right for you, then go for it! Some of us—like myself—want more, however. I'm not satisfied with even $1 million per year.

My current goal is to hit $100,000 per day, and why stop there? Think of setting goals for income like climbing a set of stairs. Step one might be making $100 per month.

Step two could be making $500. It's all arbitrary, but if the top stair is $1 million per year, you can't expect to be able to jump twenty-five stairs at once to get there. You have to climb one step at a time, and the best way to do that is by spending money.

People spend a ton of money—as much as $200,000—on university educations to obtain advanced degrees, in hopes of netting a $50,000 per year corporate job four years later, where they can work their tails off for eighty hours per week. If they land a non-salaried job, they might be lucky to get a twenty-five cent per hour raise once a year.

Meanwhile, I'm writing 500-word pieces, two to three times per week and making roughly eight times their annual salary, and I still have so much more growth ahead! Which one would you rather do? Okay, now that you've answered that, doesn't it make sense to invest even a little money in your blogging business?

I invested not only a little money in my blog, but also some time. When you run a blog, you're also an entre-preneur, so you need to meet people to promote your business. I went to some of the big box stores and handed out flyers with my blog on it. While handing them out, I would tell people about the giveaway I was doing.

It can be difficult to get people to visit your blog as a

favor or because they like your smile. However, if you offer to give them something in return for their visit, your chances of a conversion go up by a huge percentage.

GIVEAWAYS

I went to the parking lots of Target and Walmart in a lot of big cities and handed out my Instagram on a flyer with a giveaway I was doing, and it worked really well. A lot of people were surprised at the quality of the giveaways (iPhones and other tech gear), but it worked out really well for me. It didn't take a lot of money, and it was still very effective.

Incentivizing potential clients with giveaways is a great way to build a following. Just about all living things respond well to rewards; even monkeys will change their behavior for a few grapes or bananas. Humans are no different. Instead of fruit, however, you need to primarily use cash or hot technology.

I spent a decent amount of money in the beginning on giveaways. You don't have to, but it will speed up the process of follower acquisition by quite a bit if you do. I gave away a lot of $100 cash incentives and Apple products for visiting my blog, especially in the beginning. While you're out meeting people in front of the brick-and-mortar stores, make sure they know that if they follow through on visiting your website, they will have a chance to win one of these items. Tell them, "Visit my blog and you could win a new iPhone!" Then, hand them the card or flyer with your website address on it.

BUYING ADS

You can greatly accelerate the process of building a following by purchasing ads on Facebook, Instagram, and other social media sites.

Remember, your blog is a business now. Don't treat the income you get from it like it's found money; you earned it by being an entrepreneur. So, now it's time to invest some of that income back in the business, just like other entrepreneurs and business owners.

Some of the top franchises like McDonald's or Subway can cost close to a million dollars. Even most non-franchised, small businesses are going to cost $10,000-$100,000 to get off the ground.

What's worse for those business owners is that they can only advertise to people who come to their location. It doesn't do them any good to advertise their restaurant located in Dayton, Ohio to a village of people in Vietnam. With that limitation in mind, they would be lucky to reach about 10,000 people in their local vicinity.

Your blogging business, however, can target advertising dollars at people across the world if it makes sense (and it does). Blogging businesses aren't bound by the geographical limitations of retails stores, fast-food franchises, or any other brick-and-mortar operation.

Most of those businesses aren't clamoring to advertise in Vietnam, which makes the overall demand for advertising on social media sites quite low. That means that Facebook ads in that country are going to be comparatively inexpensive, and your small investment can go a long way to reach plenty of users there.

Acquiring your initial user base can be expensive. Customer acquisition through a resource like Google AdWords can have varying costs for each industry. The highly competitive industries can cost some businesses around $100 per customer.

You can work around that high up-front cost and kick-start your initial growth by purchasing ads outside of first-world countries. For example, my initial advertising efforts were in Indonesia, Vietnam, and the Philippines. The average cost per customer was two to three cents. How's that for an ROI? It sure beats the $15 per reader I would have spent for more local customer acquisitions.

Once you get that large following (social proof) from

the low-cost customers in Indonesia, the Los Angeles customers will come for free because they see so many followers on your social media platforms, which will translate to increased traffic on your site.

One of the most beautiful aspects of owning a blogging business is that no large investment is required. You can just pump in $25 here and there if that's your limit. Use money from gifts and tax returns as a good way to fuel the business. Unlike other businesses, it doesn't take much to get a blogging business off the ground.

GETTING CREATIVE

Once you start spending money on growing your business, different advertising avenues will surface in your vision. Then, you can get creative with how you market your business. Some of these more creative methods won't even cost you anything, but they can still turn into big cash returns.

FACEBOOK PIXEL

Different platforms have various nuances to them that allow you to do creative things. Take a deep dive into each one to discover some less traditional ways of keeping the money coming in.

Facebook has a piece of code you can imbed on your

website called a Facebook pixel. Relax, you don't need to be the reincarnated version of Steve Jobs to get this to work. In fact, you can get it done by watching a five-minute YouTube video. Is there anything YouTube can't teach?

Facebook's pixel allows you to track conversions, optimize ads based on data, and re-target people based on previous browsing or purchasing habits. It's an extremely powerful marketing tool for a blogger.

The ability to re-target is especially useful. If someone puts one of your proprietary products or services (like an e-course) in their cart, but never follows through with the purchase, you'll be able to re-target them. This is a red-hot lead with an even hotter conversion rate. Now, you can target that buyer with an offer like, "For a limited time, purchase this e-course for 50 percent off."

Another great benefit is that Facebook ads allow you to create *look-alike audiences,* which allows you to reach an endless amount of people who are similar to your current audience based on interests, demographics, and likes.

DISCOUNTS

Offering a discount to someone who was on the fence about buying your product is an outstanding way to close a sale. Plus, don't forget that when it comes to something with low to zero overhead, like producing an e-course, you could offer as much as 90 percent off to close the sale. If the e-course was $2,000 and you're only making $200 this way, it's still money you didn't have, and now you have a history with that buyer. Then, you can target that buyer again for a second e-course down the road, as long as the content was valuable enough to make them want to buy again.

Play liberally with discounts because most of your proprietary products and services won't cost you much to produce. Offer discounts on whatever items you sell—books, club memberships, etc.

TARGET SIMILAR BLOGS

Remember, the bigger your audience is, the more money you'll make, and another great way to build that audience is to target similar blogs in your niche.

I used to target other personal finance blogs, like *The Penny Hoarder* and *The Krazy Coupon Lady*. Both of these blogs already had millions of subscribers. In fact, *The Penny Hoarder* still makes around $30 million per year the last time I heard. The point is that these blogs have built an audience who are already buying. Therefore, it was incredibly easy for me to get in on the action. So, I posted an ad on Facebook that said, "Are you a fan of *The Penny Hoarder*? If so, you're going to love this..."

You don't always need to create your own audience. Sometimes, you can access other people's customers. It's not poaching or stealing, because they still buy from the other person anyway. You're really just doing the reader a favor by giving them another way of getting more of the same content they're already looking for.

My advice is to embrace this method and start looking for other bloggers who are already successful in your niche. Emulate their tactics and target those same readers.

REFER-A-FRIEND

A lot of companies—Uber, Lyft, Chase, Bank of America, and many more—have a refer-a-friend program. If you refer someone who signs up, you get something back. As a further bonus, whoever you bring in receives something as well. It's another fine example of a no-brainer, win-win situation.

Once you have enough followers on your blog and social media, you should definitely refer them to other businesses you use. In fact, many businesses will provide you with a dedicated link to give your customers for easy sign-up, which, if it has no income cap, is pretty much an affiliate program.

A good example of how I used the refer-a-friend tactic is when I purchased bitcoin through an app called Coinbase. I took two minutes to post a link on my Instagram and Snapchat that read, "Swipe-up to get $10 in free bitcoin." In one day, 10,000 people signed up and 1,000 of them actually bought $100 worth of bitcoin. In return, I received $10 in bitcoin for each referral and the referee received an additional $10 in bitcoin as a bonus.

Bear with me as I do some quick math again. That's $10,000 in my bank account for two minutes of work! Sure, I wouldn't have made that much money if I only had 1,000 followers, but everything in the blogosphere is set to scale. Again, the more followers you have, the more money you'll make, which is why building that initial foundation of followers is so important.

You can also look at it this way: if you've ever done cold calling or sales in any capacity, think about how long it would take to call 900,000 (roughly the current number of followers I have) people to gain 10,000 potential buyers and ultimately have the chance to close on about 1,000 of them.

If you were able to make one hundred cold calls per day

(translating to a lot of rejection and pain) while working around 250 days per year, you would reach approximately 25,000 people annually. That means it would take you about thirty-six years to call 900,000 people. Then, enjoy your retirement immediately after...if you're lucky!

The moral of the story is to think about the sheer power of reaching that many people for two minutes of work *every time* you post something. Given that there is no limit to how many posts you can create, you could easily reach an entire traditional career's worth of cold calls in about two minutes, any time, multiple times per day!

I suggest you take a moment or two now to digest that previous paragraph. It really is mind-boggling to think of how powerful social media is in reaching an enormous amount of people worldwide.

If those figures don't astound you, then you've never had a more traditional customer service, sales, or retail job. On your best day, you might be able to reach a couple hundred people per day over the phone. By blogging or using social media, you can reach 10,000 people in a miniscule fraction of the time Why would you do it any other way?

Lastly, think about this from the potential customer's perspective. Would you rather receive an unsolicited call from a random stranger about a product you've never heard of, or would you prefer to see an advertisement on an informal media outlet from someone you know very well because you've decided to follow them for a variety of reasons?

This is another example of why the modern way of leveraging social media and blogs/vlogs to reach an audience is so powerful compared to older methods like cold-calling and door-to-door sales. The more modern technique is akin to having a one-hundred-person sales team with zero cost and a better conversion rate.

Don't be afraid to tinker with the language of your refer-a-friend posts either. Try it fifty different ways if you have to. Some will work; some won't. I still change the wording of my Coinbase post. Sometimes, I try a harder sell, "Bitcoin is at an all-time low. You better swipe-up now!" Other times, I try a softer approach, "Curious about bitcoin? Swipe-up to learn more." You never know when you'll strike gold with either approach, or something in-between. The point is, don't be afraid to lose readers by offering them something through refer-a-friend. Your readers aren't going to unfollow you for this.

I recommend doing around five Google searches every so often for some keywords like "top refer-a-friend programs." In the beginning, these may not pay off quite as well as they did for me, but it's still going to be worth the few minutes it takes every day, and once you build a large enough following, boom! You will definitely keep the money coming in.

Another solid refer-a-friend opportunity is with bonuses from credit cards. If you find a good bonus program, you can do it using your own personal card. Usually, the same program will also allow you to use your business account, which, in essence, allows you to double the points. Since your blog is a business, you should do this for all the good bonus programs you find.

Credit card referral programs are especially good if you're a food or travel blogger. Since you're traveling anyway, you may as well accumulate and reap the rewards of bonus flyer miles, as well as restaurant and hotel points that will give you access to five-star accommodations and gourmet food for free.

STAY ACTIVE

As long as you keep working at your blog by either investing in the business or getting creative, you'll have a very good chance at a much better quality of life than any of your colleagues from your nine-to-five grind.

You don't need to invest 100 percent of the money you

make. As little as 10 percent might be enough to grow your business exponentially, but I recommend spending as much as 100 percent of your profit and putting it back into the business in the early days, just to get it off the ground as fast as possible.

Play around with different numbers and methods. It's your business, and you're the boss. You decide what happens and how much it grows. What's important is that you stay active.

CONCLUSION

ACT LIKE A BUSINESS

Many of my friends knew me when I was dirt poor. Today, they see me living the life of my dreams and they know it's from blogging. Yet, it's still hard for them to believe that something most people consider a hobby is making me so much money. Even stranger though, is that getting people to recognize blogging as a high-earning business isn't as hard as getting people to actually do it.

When people see how enthusiastic I am about my business and listen to the advice I give on how they can make it happen for themselves, they usually act like they're buying-in. They say, "Yeah, I see how this can work. I'm excited to get started!" Most of them understand the no-risk, no-overhead idea of it, but sadly, they never take that first step. Why, oh why don't they take that first step?

STOP PROCRASTINATING

As you read this book, it's not enough to just nod your head yes and think to yourself, "Tim makes a heck of a lot of sense here. As soon as I figure out x, y, and z, I'm going to start blogging." No! Stop procrastinating and do it now; not next week, tomorrow, or even later today! I'm serious, put the book down, or your Kindle, Nook, or iPad, and go build your social media following, or set up a hosting service like Bluehost, GoDaddy, Blogger, or one of the other half-million available choices for your blog... now! When you're done, feel free to come back and read the rest of the conclusion. What are you waiting for? Go!

Okay, so how'd it go? Did you get as many accounts as possible on social media? Did you set up a website? Did you write your first blog?

If you did any of those, congratulations! Keep that positive momentum churning and make sure you stay active. Get something done for your business every day without exception. You're well on your way to the freedom and fortune of a passive-income lifestyle. Now, for a few other things I want to mention before we say goodbye and meet up again later on in the blogosphere.

CHANGES

It is absolutely essential to immerse your business in social media as much as possible. These platforms are constantly changing, and you need to be aware of those changes as soon as they happen or you risk losing touch with your customers.

There's an easy way to monitor the evolving social media landscape. First, make sure that you install the updates when you see those tiny red numbers show up on the app icon. Second, take the two minutes necessary to read what the update does to the app. This is more important than most people realize, because sometimes the change will affect the way you need to advertise your business.

Most users just install the app without ever reading the change log, but you need to take changes like this more seriously now, because it affects more than just the way you see pictures of your first cousin's thirty-seven cats and your best friend's baby throwing his mashed carrots at the television every time he sees Ryan Seacrest. It's your business, and you need to act like it, so read the change logs of platform updates.

One example of how this helped me was my Coinbase situation. Instagram Stories implemented an update that allowed businesses to access the swipe-up feature. Initially, it was available only to those who were verified (mostly celebrities). So, if I wasn't aware of that update, I wouldn't have been able to monetize that opportunity.

It just goes to show that the type of people who respond to the question of, "How are you doing?" with "Ya know; same old, same old" will continue their same old, same old existence with less money, few options, and almost no freedom.

You need to be intentional about seeking and embracing change. While other people respond with discomfort and take years before making the leap, you should be at the forefront of change to identify and capitalize on opportunities.

Changes come faster than you realize in the social media world. Before 2007, we were all managing our Myspace pages. Then, Facebook came along, and now Instagram and Snapchat have continued the evolution. It's not going to end there either.

The next big social media thing is probably already in the works from someone sitting at a laptop in their parent's basement or a darkened college dorm room. You don't need to be the first one to jump on a new platform, but you don't want to be the last, either. There's too much money to lose while you procrastinate.

WELCOME TO THE BLOGOSPHERE

If you've read this far, you're either convinced that blogging for financial freedom is real and you're ready to get started, or for some crazy reason, you like reading well over a hundred pages about something you don't believe in. Considering the latter would be a tremendous waste of time, it's not a likely scenario, so you're probably all-in at this point and maybe you're wondering how long it takes to be successful.

Truthfully, it only took me about ten months to get my blog going, while I was working eighty hours per week with a wife and newborn at home. Of course, I had already been working on my social media accounts for two years as well.

You don't have to be all-in either. In the beginning, I was still working full-time, so I couldn't go all-in right away, but I did everything I could. I was able to monetize quickly thereafter because I had already built my social media following. Chances are, you're working a lot of hours right now too. If you can't go all-in right now, don't worry about it, but do whatever you can for now.

Don't just let the information you've acquired go to waste. Now that you have those seeds of knowledge, it's time to plant them to get your business going. Maybe you're also working eighty hours per week and have a family to care for, but you can still get a few things done to invest in your future.

As a bare minimum investment of your time, I recommend creating accounts on all the top social media platforms, and start growing them while doing your nine-to-five job. It doesn't have to be *all or nothing*, or *one or the other*.

I'm not uniquely talented or skilled in any way really, but I'm very good at the execution aspect of business. I do all those little things that others don't. Most people make a mountain out of an ant hill. A lot of what it takes to get a blog off the ground is easy, but I make sure it gets done. Now, I want you to do the same.

That's exactly how I worked my way up from being an immigrant warehouse worker surrounded by a culture of inflated diplomas and crushing debt, to a passive-income lifestyle of unmatched personal and financial freedom. The best part about my story, however, is that the same opportunity exists for everyone. All you have to do is take that first step.

The first three to six months or sometimes longer, can be difficult. You may have trouble establishing a large enough audience, but if you keep working at it and look for creative ways to grow, success *will* follow. You too can blog your way out of the rat race and into secure, stable financial freedom. If you haven't already taken my advice and got started, the time is now. See you in the blogosphere!

ABOUT THE
AUTHOR

TIMOTHY KIM epitomizes the American Dream. He was born in South Korea, but moved to Hungary with his family at the young age of five. It was a tough place to live as the only Asian family in Budapest, but through inner strength and dogged determination, Tim and his family made the best of a difficult situation.

As a young adult, Tim moved to America in 2004 to receive an education as part of his quest for a better life. He arrived with only $500 in his pocket, but once again, he found a way to confront a challenging situation and turn it into success.

Tim found an entry-level position working in the warehouse of a garage door automation company. Quickly, he began his climb up the corporate ladder until he became vice president of procurement.

Although highly successful in the corporate world, Tim left it all behind him in pursuit of bigger dreams as an online entrepreneur. Today, he is a high-income blogger and runs a highly successful financial information website, www.tubofcash.com. He also runs a club membership called the Elite Bloggers Guild where he assists others in their quest to become financially independent through blogging.

Tim prides himself on being a Christian family man. He has been married to his wife, Grace, for eight years and has a son, Josiah, who is currently age two. The future is so bright for the Kim family that Tim often claims even the sky is not the limit.

www.ingramcontent.com/pod-product-compliance
Lightning Source LLC
Chambersburg PA
CBHW031810190326
41518CB00006B/280